Tools for Teen Transformation

Perfecting Your Own Destiny

Lillie Streeter Williams

Perfecting Destiny Coaching Services

Down East
Media & Publishing

Down East Media & Publishing Services
downeastmediapublishing.com
740 Greenville Blvd. SE Suite 400-265
Greenville, NC 27858

Williams, Lillie Streeter
Tools for Teen Transformation

Published by Down East Publishing & Media Services
Original graphics designed by Down East Publishing & Media Services

Cover image by Kwazar Branding Company

ISBN: 9781693426728

PERFECTING DESTINY COACHING SERVICES, INC.
"Finding a more excellent way! "
LILLIE S. WILLIAMS, CEO
Certified Life Coach
Leadership Consultant and Transformational Speaker
https://perfectingdestiny.com/
(252)560-1952
perfectingdestinylifecoach@gmal.com
PO Box 1154, Kinston, NC 28503

SPECIAL DEDICATIONS

To Samuel, for being the best husband possible, and for allowing me time to dream night and day about this book!

To my children, Shaina Moore, and Armond Moore for all their encouragement and support of my efforts in writing this book.

To my writing coach, Celestine Davis for sharing my vision and keeping me on track.

To the thousands of students that I have had the supreme honor of working with throughout my career. Your successes will enrich my life forever.

About the Author

Lillie Streeter Williams, "Coach Lily"

Coach Lily earned her certification from the John Maxwell University in Life Coaching, Business Consulting, and Speaking. Before embarking on this prestigious certification, Mrs. Williams excelled in providing similar services for over 30 years with her expertise as an educator and school administrator. She has earned many awards including "Teacher of the Year" during her tenure as classroom teacher, Director of Education, Assistant Principal, and Principal.

Lillie conducts interactive teen empowerment training and conferences for private organizations and in her local community in which she is known affectionately as "Coach Lily." Currently, she volunteers as the Educational Chair for the Kinston-Lenoir County NAACP. In this role, Coach Lily educates parents on how to help their children to get the most from their education through community-based informational sessions and presentations. She is an ordained Elder of the Southern District Convocation of the United Holy Church of America, Inc. and a member of Faith Hope Temple UHC of Hookerton, North Carolina, where Coach Lily has served for the past 40 years. She also serves as an on-call Chaplain for UNC Lenoir Health Care hospital in Kinston, North Carolina.

She has formalized training as a Mental Health Associate. With a Bachelor of Science Degree in Special Education, a Master of Educational Administration Degree and an Advanced Degree (Ed.S.) in Educational Leadership from East Carolina University. Ms. Williams is well-versed and prepared to address all areas of leadership training and setting accountability standards. She holds a bachelor's in theological studies from Beacon University located in Columbus, Georgia. She is a woman of God that truly loves the Lord, her family and helping all people to help find "A More Excellent Way" in all areas of their lives. Coach Lily and her husband Samuel, are blessed to have five children, seven grandchildren, and one great grandchild.

About This Book

This book is written primarily for young people ages 13 through 21 years of age, but it is designed to involve the adults in their lives through every chapter.

This book is a resource for teachers and youth leaders in faith-based and educational settings. The lessons taught and the activities in this book can be adapted to various age groups to add value to the lives. The activities and messages are based on recent research, my training, and over 30 years of experience working with young people as a teacher, administrator, minister, and community leader.

This book engages the teen and young adult reader through addressing relevant issues, using realistic and authentic scenarios, practice, and short writing exercises that address issues that teens deal with on an everyday basis. It is an authoritative framework of workable options which encourages teens to make life-affirming choices so that they may succeed in all areas of their lives. This book invites teens to engage their parents and other adults in this learning process on their way to self-reliance.

After digesting its contents and applying the tools within the instructional activities in *Tools for Teen Transformation*, teens, parents, pastors, teachers, and others have reported markedly transformational thinking and behavioral changes in the teens they know.

As a result of using the "tools" in this book...

- Teens will learn how to love themselves.
- Teens will learn how to make better decisions.
- Teens will learn methods to manage their relationships.
- Teens will learn tools for better communication.
- Teens will decrease defiant behaviors.
- Teens will have tools to increase their self-esteem and avoid drug and alcohol abuse.

    And parents will sleep better at night.

These tools will help bring generations closer together by giving parents or guardians, grandparents and even great grandparents talking points and opportunities for interacting with their teens and young adults

Contents

Let's begin!

Chapter 1
Don't Let *Them* in Your Head

Your head is the residence of your brain. According to the experts, your brain is one of the largest and most complex organs in the human body with over 100 billion nerves that communicate in trillions of connections. The brain is made up of many specialized areas. They all work together to create each unique individual. What goes on inside our brains affect how we function on every level.

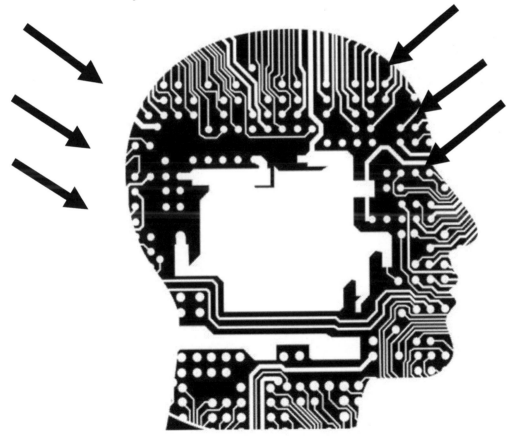

When I talk about your head, I'm talking about your mind and all the thoughts, ideas, emotions, and belief systems that make you who you are. When all these things, positive or negative, come together, they will cause you to behave in a certain way. We all hope to have positive thoughts and influences because they make us feel good about ourselves and our lives. We all want to surround ourselves with positive people who support us during our successes and our challenges. But that is not always going be the situation. As the character, Forrest Gump in the movie of the same name reminds us, "Life is like a box of chocolates, you never know what you're going to get." So, you must learn to confront negative situations and negative people.

Negative thoughts and negative people

What about the negative thoughts and the people who do not support you? Negative thoughts will cause you to act, say, and believe things that do not build your self-esteem, make you feel inadequate, or feel overly sensitive. Negative acts do not add value to you. They are anything that hurts you or anybody else, like name-calling, teasing and bullying. Negative thoughts can make you exaggerate the importance of one painful event , so you will shut down whenever you meet similar obstacles or challenges.

Guard your thoughts against all negativity, including those that are coming from social media. Social media is one of the most significant and easiest ways to receive negativity. But it's also the one avenue you have absolute control over if you choose to do so. Take the challenge to unplug from all negativity. Learn how to use all the tools social media platforms provide to isolate yourself from trolls and agitators that hinder your peace of mind.

The world is full of people who will try to make you feel anxious, unworthy, or just plain bad about who you are or what you do. Who are these people? They are not always the enemies we can quickly identify. They can be anybody: sisters, brothers, neighbors, teachers, or even your best friend. People you care about can sometimes create the most negativity in your life...if you let them.

How do negative thoughts operate, anyway?

They have a negative impact on every aspect of your life if you *let* them in your head. To guard against them, fill your head with thoughts that will benefit you, and counter any new negative ideas with new positive ones.

Problems and Solutions

How can you keep negative thoughts and ideas out of your head? What kind of thoughts should you allow in your head that will keep you in your "A" game?

How can you be happy all this week, excel in all your classes, and forgive yourself for anything you let in your head last week that kept you from being your best self?!

1. Fill your subconscious mind with positive thoughts. Focus on the good things in life. Start with any good relationships you have with families or friends. Then add physical things like sunshine, etc. You can stop right there or move on to things that are even more specific to you such as passing that science test or buying a new pair of shoes. What other positive feelings or experiences can you think of?

2. Don't personalize situations when bad or sad things happen. Don't internalize blame that is not yours to keep. You have no control over other people's actions and many circumstances are not in your control.

3. Don't see everything as either black or white. You don't have to be perfect! There is no such thing as a perfect life. Your attitude and ability to handle all aspects of life makes all the difference.

4. Create and recite daily affirmations to replace your negative self-talk:

- I am smart and beautiful, or I am smart and handsome.

- I am going to have a fantastic week at school.

- I will complete every task that I am given.

- I am happy being me!

Let's Summarize

Number 1: Don't let negative thoughts come in and stay in your head.

Number 2: Choose to be positive.

Number 3: Counter all negative thoughts with positive alternatives that support you and that more accurately reflect your true potential.

Teen Assignment

Dwell on positive thoughts. Accept yourself and recognize all your great qualities. You can make that choice! Use index cards or a sticky note pad to write affirmations that will directly counter or go against any negative thoughts, feelings, or beliefs you have now. Write additional ones as new challenges arise. Place them where you will most likely see them during your daily routine, such as around your mirror, in your locker, inside your homework binder, or in your phone. When that is not possible, try using a visual reminder such as a picture, a ribbon, a rubber band, or anything that will trigger you to recall your affirmation for the day. You get the idea!

Now, ask yourself, "How can I build someone else up? Then, just do it! When you become more of a giver, you will grow in the path you have chosen.

 **Parent-Teen Share**

The sample below is for teens, but parents and other adults have negative thoughts too! Take a piece of paper and draw a line down the middle. On one side, write "Negative Thoughts. " On the other side, write "Alternative Positive Thoughts." You can use the template provided after this sample for practice and to make copies for future use.

Negative Thoughts	Alternative Positive Thoughts
I am not popular.	There are people who care about me and love my company.
I am not good at school.	My desire for learning is great.
I do not have the latest style of clothing.	I can find ways to be creative with the clothes I have.
I am too sad to succeed.	I give myself permission to feel happy and at ease with my life.

It is not productive to deny negative thoughts, but we can and must change our relationship with them. Instead of letting negativity hinder your progress, redirect its energy. Let it fuel your sense of purpose and your resolve to succeed. You can choose to look at negative thoughts differently by allowing them to fuel your decisions to adopt positive alternatives. Don't let negative thoughts and ideas rule you. You can rule them instead!

Replacing the Negative with **the Positive!**

My Negative Thoughts	Alternative Positive Thoughts

Chapter 2

I Love Me,

I Love Me,

I Love Me!

> *Loving yourself...does not mean being self-absorbed or narcissistic, or disregarding others. Rather it means welcoming yourself as the most honored guest in your own heart, a guest worthy of respect, a lovable companion.* —Margo Anand

So many times, we wake up tired and unrefreshed, and we almost immediately begin to dread the day that lies ahead. Your inner voice may complain, "It's too early! I feel like I just laid down. Just a few minutes more... I need just a few minutes more." But you know how that day will probably unfold if you listen to that voice.

Nevertheless, it's time to get on up. As you recall all the messes and mishaps from the previous days and weeks, your heart begins to sink, and you start to feel helpless and incompetent. This may have been a recurring storyline in your life, but there is good news! It does not have to be.

You have the ability to create a better day today and for all the days in your future. Past mistakes should not continue to darken your future. Do not let regret cast a shadow upon your "now" moments. There are specific ways to change your mindset for you to have an enjoyable day at school or work and be your best self yet! You can make this week a better week than last week if you just remember to love yourself!

What does "loving yourself" look like? What better choices can you make and what positive behaviors can you do to show yourself more love?

Start with a little positive self-talk. In this case, I am talking about a positive statement that describes a desired situation or goal that you repeat over and over again.

Positive self-talk can be accomplished with your inner voice but speaking aloud can often be more powerful. If you think it, you speak it, you hear it, and you will believe it! Hearing positive messages from your own voice is powerful! Turning your self-talk into affirmations gets into your subconscious mind and can work for you in a mighty way.

Say to yourself, "It's personal, it's all about me this morning!"

"I can do what makes me feel happy, competent, and whole."

Say it until you mean it! Now, break into your Happy Dance, and shout, "Oh, how I love Me! I affirm this truth...I love me!"

Problems and Solutions

How can you focus on yourself without becoming narcissistic or getting a *big head*?

Begin by acknowledging all the effort and the good-will that others have contributed to your success. Build a realistic attitude about your successes as well as your challenges. What you think of as failure is often part of the learning process that will help you fine-tune your approach to the changes you need to make. For example, if you find that you cannot make a sports team, think about other ways to stay involved. You may have an opportunity in the future, or you could just find that you may enjoy another position with the team even more. Your attitude about yourself and life's challenges is everything! Develop a mindset for success. Be willing to adapt when things don't go just as you planned. Learn strategies for staying focused and motivated such as writing your goals down, talking with interested adults, and associating with peers who have similar goals. School clubs and some community groups are suitable places to start. Ask your school counselor, teachers, parents, trusted friends and other adults for referrals and feedback.

📝 Teen Assignment

First, read the samples then practice writing your own in the space provided.

Sample Affirmations # 1

Because I Love Me …

- I can't hang out with you (Say the names) if you are hanging out in the wrong place with the wrong crowd of people.
- I will not consume drugs, alcohol or anything that will alter my clear thinking or mess up my mind.
- I'm doing all I can do today, right now, to add value to the people around me and to make my future a good place to be.
- I will ask for and accept help from qualified persons to overcome any difficulties that I am having.

Sample Affirmations # 2

I love and respect myself sooo much that…

- I am going to love and respect others (parents, teachers, adults, students, and co-workers).

- I'm going to teach others how to love and respect themselves by watching me!
- I'm going to make choices and act in ways that others will respect me too.
- I will follow the rules put in place to keep me safe.

Practice writing your own affirmations below.

#1. Because *I Love* me ...

_____

_____

_____

#2. *I Love* and respect myself so much that ...

_____

_____

_____

How will you know you love yourself?

The answer is that you and everyone else will see changes in your behavior, your attitude, and your level of happiness.

Put your affirmations where you cannot miss them: on your mirror, in your journal, on the door of your school locker, in your bible, in your phone, on the refrigerator, etc. Place them all over the place! Create short ones, long ones, and secret ones that only you will understand. Place them somewhere that you can't miss them.

Create affirmations to address all areas of your life. You must be honest with yourself to make real and lasting changes.

 **Parent-Teen Share**

Start by making short, middle, and long-term goals. Set your priorities for reaching *your* goals as a basis for how *you* plan to use *your* time. If you do not know how to begin, talk it over with your parents or guardians. Be sure to share your goals with them. They may be able to identify and provide resources or see options that you do not know about yet. They may even be able to remove some obstacles if they know where you are headed.

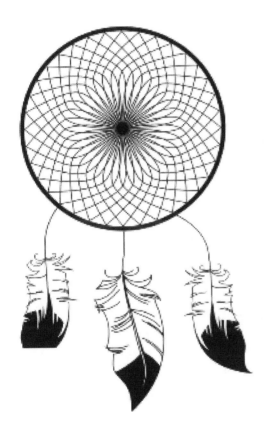

A goal without a plan is just a dream.

My Goals

	Name: _____ Date: _____

My Goal	Time Frame	Steps to take	Who can help?

Chapter 3

Gratitude: Your Superpower!

You made it through the weekend, you made it through last week, last month, and last year. However, take nothing for granted. Instead, adopt an attitude of gratitude. Gratitude is more than saying, "Thank you." It is a lifestyle. In comic books and sci-fi movies, superpowers allow seemingly ordinary people to transform into beings that can change the physical and sometimes the nonphysical world. Intentional gratitude can be your superpower. To live a life of gratitude means to be grateful on purpose and with intention. Being thankful can be your superpower to help you live happier, healthier, and longer!

You can start developing this superpower immediately, right where you are, right now. No costume or telephone booth is required. You don't even need a sidekick. Transform your attitude to transform your life. Become your own superhero!

How does it work?

What happens when you become intentionally thankful and full of gratitude? Gratitude makes us happier and makes others happier with us! Gratitude makes you less envious, less stressed, and more willing to take on new activities with new possibilities for your life.

By practicing gratitude, you will become more trusting, more social, and more appreciative. As a result, you will deepen and improve your relationships. You will make more friends. You will have the power to create a better world for yourself, your family, your school, and your community.

Why should you be intentionally grateful?

There has been evidence to support that when we write down emotionally positive sentences, we can expect better health, better performance, and we can significantly increase our lifespan according to what has become known as The Nun Study.[1] During this study, researchers came across essays written by nuns over a long period of time. Based on the analysis of their writings and the lives of the nuns that wrote them, the researchers proved that when you write down happy thoughts, you will be healthier, more satisfied with your life, and live longer! You can benefit from that same principle in your life.

While it's understandable that nobody can be positive 100% of the time, you have the absolute power to practice gratitude. As this practice becomes a regular part of your life, you are going to feel better, and you will create positive emotions. As a result, more of the good things that you are grateful for will come to you.

How can you practice intentional gratitude?

There are actions and practices that you can choose to become more grateful. Before you get up and start your day, think about all the things that you appreciate: what you see, smell, hear, feel, and so on at that moment. Let this be a daily habit for the best results.

Create a gratitude notebook or include statements of gratitude with your daily affirmations. Write down things that make you feel grateful during your day as they come to mind. Is it your family, your friends, good grades, good health, a sound mind, a place to live, food to eat, clothes to wear, a job, and some great teachers? Although your list can be similar to another person, make sure it reflects what you are particularly grateful for. Then meditate on those things.

Getting Focused

This meditation is not a hocus-pocus activity, but it requires setting aside time for focused thinking. It does not require repetitive words, but it does require you to focus on the things that make you feel grateful. Take it further by meditating on those things that may not be as you want them. Be thankful that they are coming or getting into place. This will help you to develop a mindset of expectation and create a space for good things to continue to happen. It is a simple practice of taking a few minutes to think about real possibilities for your life. This kind of focus can boost your mood, help you focus on the positive outcomes, and brighten your mood all day. Besides, the reality is that when you focus on the good things that you want; you will make choices and behave in a way that will most likely bring those things into your future.

Sharing Your Superpower

Go tell someone about it! Let those in your life know what you appreciate about them. Be truthful, but don't use any "buts," such as, "I appreciate you for helping with my science project, *but* you could have helped me more with the poster." Express your gratitude vocally or in a note that will be easily discovered. You may be the only person that day, week, month, or year, that has given someone any kudos. The goodwill will benefit you both. This boomerang effect is a real superpower phenomenon!

Hangout with others who practice gratefulness. Create a grateful crew or a Gratefulness Universe! Superheroes tend to hang together, right? Consider suggesting that words or acts of thankfulness become a practice in the organizations or clubs that you already belong. Meditate or focus on a spirit of thankfulness. Take a few minutes a day to think about who and what you are thankful for. Visualize a life with all your emotional, physical, spiritual, and financial needs being met.

Problems and Solutions

Did something terrible or unfortunate happen? How could it have been worst? Believe me, no matter how bad it seems, it could have been worst! There is always a tomorrow to improve any situation.

What if you can't think of anything to be thankful for at that moment? Start with the more obvious and visible aspects of your life, such as your physical life then transport your thinking to other areas of your life.

- I am thankful for my health.

- I am thankful for food to eat.

- I am thankful for people who love me.

- I am thankful that I have other options.

- I am thankful for my ability to_____.

- I am thankful for the great life that I am preparing for right now.

Gratitude can change your viewpoint and transform your life!

~ Coach Lily

Number 1: Create a separate gratitude notebook or include statements of gratitude with your daily affirmations.

Number 2: Meditate or focus on a spirit of thankfulness. Take a few minutes a day to think about who and what you are thankful for such as a life with all your basic needs met. Focus on positive outcomes that may not even exist as though they will.

Number 3: Express it out loud. Tell someone you are grateful for their contribution to your life or the lives of others.

Number 4: Hangout with others who practice gratefulness. Create or find a space to surround yourself with people you appreciate and that appreciate you.

📝 Teen Assignment

Remember sharing what you are thankful for isn't just for Thanksgiving. Set a time of day to meditate on being grateful and write in your gratitude journal every day! Make a habit of expressing your gratitude to the people in your life such as your friends, siblings, parents, teachers, or any other person in your life. This will take some pre-thinking but be authentic. Think of ways that you can practice gratitude every day.

💡 Parent-Teen Share

Write a list of 5 things that you are grateful for and share them with each other. They do not have to involve each other, but a few that do will go a long way. However, sharing your gratitude for things and people in other areas of your life such as work, school, church, or your neighborhood, will give you an opportunity to know each other on a different level. Listen and acknowledge each other with your words and body language. End this session by thanking each other for sharing.

"Gratitude opens the door to the power, the wisdom, the creativity of the universe. You open the door through gratitude."
— Deepak Chopra

1. Danner, Deborah D, David A. Snowdon, and Wallace V. Freisen. "Positive Emotions in Early Life and Longevity: Findings from the Nun Study." *Journal of Personality and Social Psychology*, vol. 80, no. 5, 2001, pp. 804–813., doi:10.1037//0022-3514.80.5.804.

Chapter 4

Flexing Your Emotional Muscles

Where are all these emotions coming from, anyway?

Like the rest of the human population, as a teen, you experience lots of emotions. You may not be able to put a name on what you are feeling or why you are feeling a certain way, at least not all the time. Emotions can run from one extreme to another with highs and lows of feeling happy, sad, anxious, bored, curious, excited, and depressed, to name a very few. Some of the issues are related to physical changes or hormones. Changes in your life can intensify your emotions. As you become a teen, you are also approaching adulthood, which usually leads to more significant responsibilities and new expectations. This can result in added pressure from others and yourself. Be assured that there are social and scientific explanations for why you have such emotional rollercoaster rides. It is perfectly natural at this stage in your life! You may be experiencing emotional roller coasters because life issues and your body are changing your emotional state. As you experience these predictable changes, you may also experience many uncontrollable social ones.

Now what?

You must learn when and how to flex your emotional muscles in ways that will be more beneficial and less damaging to you and others. It will be up to you to independently make the best and most responsible decisions that you can. There will be times when it will be wise to ask for help. When you can accept and embrace the fact that you may need help, you really are growing up. By seeking help, you are taking greater responsibility for how your life turns out. As you grow older, knowing when to seek advice will benefit you greatly.

First, you must develop skills to manage your emotions. Start with identifying your feelings. If you cannot put them into words, then maybe you shouldn't act upon your feelings until you can. If you are struggling to name your emotion, it's a good thing to have a reliable go-to method that will limit their harmful consequences to you and possibly others.

Let me tell you a story about a high school freshman named Marcus, who had some choices to make.

Marcus' Story

Marcus became agitated every time he was asked to go to the board to show his work for a math problem. Although he completed all his work and he was sure that it was correct, there was that "feeling" every time. Eventually, he began to talk back to the teacher or crack a joke to disrupt class every time he was asked to go to the board. He knew he was going down a path that would have negative consequences. He knew he had to make a change.

After Marcus took the time to think his problem through, he realized that that feeling he experienced was embarrassment. He admitted that much to himself, but then he had to figure out why. Although he appeared outgoing and studious, what Marcus wanted most of all was to be "cool." In his mind, cool people did not cooperate, and they surely did not come up with all the right answers. When many of his at-home privileges began fading away due to the reports of his behavior to his parents, Marcus was forced to rethink his actions and the emotions behind them. He decided to make a change. After promising to improve, Marcus came up with a plan. He decided to make a deal with a friend to go up with him to the board. Then he called out two other students and formed a competition. Before long all the students were competing for bragging rights and the pressure was off Marcus. He flexed his emotions but turned them towards better responses and avoided the negative ones.

Marcus' plan of Action may have looked like the one below.

Emotions	Negative Responses	Better Responses
• *Embarrassment* • *Lack of-confidence* • *Fear of rejection: Peer Pressure*	• Uncooperative • Disrupt class • Shame	• Meet privately with teacher. • Buddy-up (Seek help from a classmate) • Make it fun!

Teens (and some adults) find it difficult to acknowledge what they are feeling, or perhaps they simply don't know how to identify their feelings. If this does not come easy for you, then practice. Stop and take the time to ask yourself what you are feeling and why, when you notice a shift in your emotions. What is happening? Where are you? Who is around you? Make a note in your journal if it is not clear to you. Eventually, you will see a pattern that can help you identify what you were feeling and why. Once you can identify and understand the basis of your feelings, your vulnerability may come into play. If it does, it is natural to have a fear of rejection. As a result, you may use any items on this list as a defense mechanism or as strategies to protect yourself. Which of these strategies do you use when you feel emotionally threatened? Place a check beside all that apply. Add others as needed.

being overly critical	
being too defensive	
blaming others	
shutting down	
displaying anger	
intimidation	
cry	
yell	
whine	

So, what?

Emotions are a natural part of life. They are one of the most beautiful things about being a human being. Emotions can protect us and enhance our lives, but if certain emotions or feelings are unchecked and unmanaged, they can cause severe harm. As a teen, your life may, at times, feel like an emotional roller coaster ride. There are so many new experiences and new choices that can make your emotions hard to manage.

Keep in mind that there are no bad emotions! The intensity of emotions may vary based on many factors and the situation you are facing at the time. Sometimes, people you know may be experiencing similar issues, but seem to be dealing with their emotions a lot better. The keyword is "seems!" If you are in poor physical health, suffered multiple losses or disappointments, or have been under stress for a long time, your emotions can seem unbearable.

It is not productive to beat yourself up about what you are feeling. Emotions can come and go in a flash. However, when you have feelings that won't go away, make you feel bad about yourself, disturb your relationships, and affects your health, you need to discover why you have those feelings. Although, you can work out some emotional issues on your own, there are times that you may need help.

The worst thing you can do is to deny yourself help when you need it. Rejecting and holding your feelings inside can lead to long-term mental and physical health problems. Take care of your emotional and mental health. Ask for help from a parent, a friend, teacher, pastor, or counselor when unhealthy feelings stay around longer than usual. As you receive emotional support, flex your emotional muscles by doing things that give you joy and peace every chance you have.

Problems and Solutions

When depression or the blues seem to linger and you just can't shake it off, and it begins to affect all areas of your life, you may need professional help.

Getting help as soon as possible is the key to helping you recover from traumatic circumstances including the death of a friend or loved one, sexual crime or other victimization, legal problems, constant anxiety, self-esteem concerns, family issues, or other persistent problems that you cannot handle on your own.

For affordable, local help there are in-school services for teens and college students. Some community counselors or therapists offer sliding fee services that are based on the ability to pay, and some agencies offer free services. If unsure, ask for and verify that a counselor or therapist is certified by the state in which they operate.

Two National Resources

National Suicide Prevention Lifeline https://suicidepreventionlifeline.org/ 1-800-273-TALK **(8255)**	A national network of local crisis centers. It provides free and confidential emotional support to people in suicidal crisis or emotional distress 24 hours a day, 7 days a week for all types of reasons.
The Trevor Project www.TheTrevorProject.org 1--866-4-U-TREVOR **(7386)** Talk, Chat, or Text	Around-the-clock crisis and suicide prevention helpline for lesbian, gay, bisexual, transgender and questioning (LGBTQ) youth under 25. Available as a resource to parents, family members and friends of young people.

Let's Summarize

According to the American Foundation for Suicide Prevention, you may need help from a therapist if you participate in any of these behaviors. [2]

1. Self-Harm
2. Chronic Substance Abuse
3. Thinking about, talking about, and attempting suicide

Don't deny what you see and experience. If you or anyone you know who is exhibiting this behavior, report it so you or they can receive help. If not taken seriously, these behaviors can lead to permanent damage or death. If you are afraid to report it, first seek out help anonymously, but get help. Your life or the life of another may depend on it.

Teen Assignment

Practice some coping techniques by helping "Jan" to flex and manage her emotions.

Jan's Story

Jan panics whenever she enters the cafeteria alone. Her face feels hot, and her throat tightens. Jan hugs her purse and any books she is carrying close to her body like a shield. She looks around the room, careful to avoid the eyes of everyone. Most of her friends have an earlier lunch period and is gone when Jan arrives. So, she often avoids the cafeteria altogether or goes through the line and then dashes out the door to eat on a nearby step, even in bad weather.

What can Jan do to manage her emotions better?

_____

_____

_____

_____

_____

_____

_____

Think and Prepare!
How you can take control of your emotions and behavior?
Flexing your Emotional Muscles Activity

Think before you react! For each entry, think about who can help you find better solutions for any emotional responses you want to change such as parents, teacher, friends, self-action or self-affirmation.

EMOTION	NEGATIVE RESPONSE	BETTER RESPONSE
Anger	Break something. Yell and call names. Make threats.	Breathe and count to ten. Focus on my happy place. If possible, walk away. Call someone before I do something "stupid."

💡 Parent-Teen Share

Work through some scenarios together. Sometime the best offense is a great defense. Take turns sharing an experience that you handled in the past. Each person can share their story then take turns asking each other the questions below. Feel free to come up with some other non-judgmental questions for clarification purposes. Note to Parents: This is not a time to lecture but a time to listen and guide.

- What emotion or emotions did you feel?
- Were these emotions based on a previous experience?
- How did you react?
- How do you wish you had reacted?
- What are some other choices you could have made?
- What changes can you make in your thinking and reactions to "fight" or redirect those emotions for a better outcome?

Think of some long-term alternatives or solutions, so that you will be ready next time. Work together because two heads a better than one.

2. "Risk Factors and Warning Signs." AFSP. 14 Nov. 2018. American Foundation for Suicide Prevention. 15 May 2019 <https://afsp.org/about-suicide/risk-factors-and-warning-signs/>.

Chapter 5

Listening and Being Heard

♬You know parents are the same ...There's no need to argue ... Parents just don't understand ♬

by Jazzy Jeff and The Fresh Prince [3]

In some families, teens and parents suffer a breakdown in communication in what some call the generation gap. Some experts believe this gap is not a certainty, but it's mostly fueled by the media. When we become teens, we do not automatically rebel against our parents' values or the authority of the culture we live in.

Yes, a few changes take place between generations. Also, some parents seem to forget what it was like to be a teen. With thoughtful consideration and meaningful communication, we can close much of this so-called generation gap.

All relationships have ups and downs. Sometimes we feel frustrated or hurt. Sometimes we just don't feel that anyone hears us. This feeling is fixable if we care enough to take deliberate, intentional steps. A good relationship with your parents or guardians can be the key to your success in life. No one will have as much invested in your development and your success. Others might love you, but no one has been in the position to see you at your most vulnerable state, seen you at your worst, still believe in you, and be absolutely committed to having you achieve the best outcome for your life.

However, family relationships, like any long-term relationship, can have a history of awkward conversations about touchy subjects. For you to honestly hear each other or communicate, you must commit to the idea that the feelings of each of you are valid. While your feelings are real, you must also commit to the notion that the other person's feelings are just as *real* as yours.

This commitment is the basis of "intentional dialogue." Over time, you will begin to believe the other person is not wrong; it is just the way they feel, period. In the article "Relationship Salve," Leo Babauta, a relationship guru, explains that when we get into an argument, we frequently make our loved ones feel like they're wrong.[4] Many times, we offer a peace offering, but follow up with a right hook such as, "I can see why you feel that way, but..." *Do not offer any "buts."* When we include a" but" or otherwise criticize their feelings, you are still saying that they're wrong.[3] That little word, "but," can completely shut down open communication.

Intentional Dialogue Activity

Intentional dialogue is a set of rules for listening and sharing your feelings. When you and your parents engage in "intentional dialogue," it provides the opportunity for you to hear and understand each other clearly and more fully. Set enough time aside in a space where you will not be disturbed. That is important. Also, do not schedule anything for an exact time directly following this exchange or you may disrupt the communication and forfeit its benefits. You need to be all-in and not thinking about the next thing.

Rules of Engagement

Set aside your feelings for a moment and listen to understand what the other person is saying. Try not to fall into old patterns of thinking you know what they are going to say.

Here are some general guidelines.

- ♥ Listen as though you've never heard them before.
- ♥ Share experiences in ways that are real and personal.
- ♥ No "what if" scenarios that involve imaginary friends.
- ♥ Be honest but not brutal. Remember you love each other.
- ♥ Some risk is involved, so be kind.

The acts of listening and sharing without our typical rush to judgment can foster understanding and connection between children and parents. Intentional dialogue can be a powerful tool to heal wounds and avoid disastrous acting-out. I suggest that in the parent-teen partnership that the teen be the first to begin each step. This activity can be a great exercise between parents, friends, and co-workers too! The four steps explained below: mirroring, validating, empathizing, and giving a gift are adapted from relationship expert Harvell's "Three Steps to Intentional Dialogue."

Step 1: Mirroring Exercise

Mirroring is listening without distorting the thoughts and feelings of each other. The first step of an intentional dialogue is to mirror your parent/teen and try to hear each other without judgment. Follow the basic script below. One person will be the sharer and the other the receiver.

1. The sharer will convey the message that they would like the parent or teen to hear. Start with "I" and describe your feelings. For example, "I feel hurt when you make fun of how I dress."

2. The receiver of the message then mirrors the message of the sharer. For example, "If I got it, let me know. You feel hurt when I tell you that you don't know how to dress. Did I get it right?"

3. The sharer will repeat or explain their message until it is received.

   When the exchange is complete, the receiver says, "Is there more about that?" By asking this question, the receiver provides the sharer with the opportunity to reveal their feelings more fully and prevents receivers from responding to incomplete messages.

4. The receiver of the message (parent or teen), then summarizes the complete message.

   For example, the receiver may start with, "Let me see if I got that right, you said..."

5. Then the receiver will check for accuracy with, "Did I get it all?"

Step 2: Validating Exercise

Why is it not enough just to listen? You must learn to pay close attention to understand your partner's truth. "It's not enough just to be heard," says Dr. Harville Hendrix.[5] Your teen or parent want to know, "'Do you see that I'm not crazy?'"

- The parent or teen does not have to agree with the argument of their dialogue partner, but they should validate it.
- Use sentences like this: "You make sense because ..." or "I can see what you're saying ..." Using these kinds of phrases tells your dialogue partner that you value their feelings.
- Your parent or teen must make certain that the speaker feels validated before moving on. If they do, move on to the next step.

Step 3: Empathizing Exercise

Once the feeling is expressed, it's time to put yourself in your partner's shoes. Try to understand what they are feeling by imagining how you would feel in the same circumstances from their point of view. *Go* to that place with him or her for a moment. This can be a <u>moment of great connection.</u>

<u>How to do it...</u>

- Start with a statement such as, "I can imagine that you might be feeling..."

or "I can see that you are feeling...."

- Check to make sure that the feeling you imagine is true.
- When your partner gives you a thumbs up, reverse and give them a turn.

Step 4: Giving the Gift

It's time to ask your partner for a small, positive offering.

The Gift Exercise

- The receiver will make a simple request like, "Right now, can I make a request?"

  Some Examples

  - "Can you come and hug me?
  - "Can you say a kind word to me?"

- Your partner should fulfill your request, then switch to give them the same opportunity.
- Keep working at giving each other "gifts" until a shift occurs. The goal is to keep going until you see each other without judgment.

Use your smartphone to scan the QR code or follow the link to see an intentional dialogue in practice.

View Intentional Dialogue Practice

https://youtu.be/m82EXFcPBa8

Problems and Solutions

Problem: There are barriers to getting enough face-to-face alone time with your parent or guardian.

Solution: Try Facebook Messenger, Skype, Zoom, Face Time, or some other video communication or sharing platform.

Let's Summarize

Communication is fundamental

Communication is a must for all successful relationships. It is never too early to learn to be an effective communicator, which means you know how to express yourself and you know how to listen to others. It also means you know how to respond in ways that keep the lines of communication open for the future.

Intentional dialogue, whether it's formal or informal, is one way to keep lines of communication open. Be sure to follow the rules and take turns sharing and receiving.

Don't be disappointed if your first attempt is a bit of a struggle. This is a process that gets better if you stick with it. So, plan another one to address another issue on your list or something new as it comes up. Sometimes you will get better results than others, but each conversation should allow you to know each other better and trust each other more with your feelings.

Teen Assignment

Make a list of 5 to 7 things you want your parents to understand about you, something you do or would like to do. Let's call them the "To Understands" and the "To Do's." Cluster the similar "To Understands and "To Do's" in categories. Are they about trust, safety, freedom, self-reliance, education, reputation, and so on? Do you see a pattern? Make a note or color code any patterns you see. Then prioritize the groupings based on their importance or how much they stress your relationship. Identify which one would make the greatest change, create the best understanding, and lead to more ease between you and your parents. Choose the one that is the top of your list for an intentional dialogue.

This may be someone's general list of concerns.

1. I can't choose what I eat.
2. Charlie or Suzy gets more attention because he/she whines, but you tell me not to whine.
3. I want to dress more like my friends.
4. You say I can't cook, but you never let me try.
5. I want to choose my own after-school activities.
6. I want you to spend more time talking to me instead of just telling me what to do.
7. I need a car, so I won't have to wait on anybody.
8. I want a job, so I can buy more of the things I like.
9. You do not listen to me.
10. I don't have any real friends and you don't seem to care.

Now, color code or arrange them based on what they have in common or how they connect.

- Items 4, 5, and 8 seem to be more about self-reliance.
- Items 2, 6, and 9 seem to be more about building a stronger bond or relationship.
- Items 1, 5, and 7 seem to be more about independence.

There is no right or wrong way to group your list of concerns but going through this process will allow you to understand yourself better. It also will give you a way to express your feelings to others.

Now, following the scenario above, you could decide which topic is the most important to you at this moment: self-reliance, building a stronger bond, or independence. Then decide where you want to begin. Do you want to address how they can best assist you in being more self-reliant? Or, do you want to start by building a stronger bond through communication? Is being more independent higher on your agenda at this moment?

Ask your parents to set aside an afternoon when they will have little restraints on their time. It may take a few minutes or an hour. How long it takes is how long it takes. With practice, you will both know what to expect.

Your Action Plan

- Explain to your parents that you want to talk with them in a unique way called intentional dialogue.
- Share the steps that you will take: Mirroring, Validating, Empathizing followed by the Giving of Gifts. You can let them read the description in your book, but practice explaining it in your own way.
- Set a time and place in which you are both less likely to be disturbed. Then, do it!

Communication Guidelines: Making a Request

Think about the specific goals that you want to accomplish in different areas of your life. Focus on a particular goal, its purpose, and the action you wish your parents or guardians to take to help you reach that goal. Remember, your objective is to gain an ally and not to win an argument. Unlike what you may see on television, an appropriate or good time to talk is not when there are lots of distractions. You want to build your credibility for the long term. Tricking your parents or guardian into saying "yes" will not be beneficial to you. You must be open to hearing what they have to say. They may have a better solution than you can even imagine for whatever you are hoping for! Also, remember that "No," could mean "just not right now." Always be respectful and polite. Often, it's not what you say but how you say it.

 Parent-Teen Share

After the intentional dialogue is complete, let writing a note of gratitude to each other be part of your "gifting." Or you can share a special affirmation to commemorate the event verbally. Nothing elaborate but make honest, heart-felt statements like: "I appreciate who you are to me." "I want to thank you for sharing and listening to me today." "If I had to choose a parent/child, I would choose you."

Write your own "to understand" and "to do' lists to begin.

TO UNDERSTAND	TO DO

3. Parents Just Don't Understand by DJ Jazzy Jeff & the Fresh Prince (Jeff Townes and Will Smith), won the 1989 Grammy for Best Rap Performance.
4. Leo Babauta's "Relationship Salve: The Practice of Intentional Dialogues" found at zenhabits.net
5. Dr. Harville Hendrix is the creator of Imago Relationship Therapy and is best known for his book *Getting the Love You Want*, a New York Times best-seller.

Chapter 6
Police Yourself

When THEY Know you!

From early childhood, we begin to test our boundaries. Whether it's our parents, teachers or others placed in charge, the purpose of their authority is to protect younger people. That's you! The authority of this inner circle of adults with parental or parent-like authority rests on two foundations: leadership and instruction. In both cases, your *inner-circle-adults* are striving to affect the choices you make now and prepare you to make choices on your own when they are not around. They want and need to have this influence to support the enormous responsibility they have assumed for your daily care and healthy growth.

#It'sNotToRuinYourLife!

Under normal conditions, until around 9 or 10 years old, it probably seemed relatively easy to follow the leadership and authority of your parents. But beginning as early as 9, as you entered adolescence, something changed. You began to challenge your parents' leadership and their instructions. This is normal, but depending upon your culture or your specific parents, how outwardly you begin that questioning process may vary. However, some type of confrontations and defiant behavior will usually start just the same. It may begin with questioning. "Why, do I?" "Why should I?' Then escalate to, "I don't have to!" "You can't make me!" Then move on to, "It's my life!"

Underlying some of these constant arguments may be your need to know a "good" reason for following instructions. And sometimes, you may simply want to test the boundaries with a statement like, "I'll do it later!" The adults in authority may wonder what happened to that cooperative, "sweet" child that you use to be. Even you may not know! You do not have to wait to understand why you feel the way you do to begin to control your behavior.

In some families, the rules for certain aspects of your life may be automatically expected at specific ages. In other families, it must be negotiated. Whatever skills you use to negotiate with your parents and guardians usually spill over to teachers and other adults who have a long-term personal stake in the adult you will become. So, do not rely on trickery or outright lies. Let your skills be based on traits that will bring you honor and not shame.

If you develop a good reputation with your parents, guardians, teachers, or other adults trusted with authority over you, that can be a big plus. As remarkable as it seems, simply being reasonable and reliable will allow you to develop trusting relationships that can result in a happier life for you. It can be a minus if you rebel just for rebelling sake. Your *inner-circle-adults* will not be happy and ultimately, you won't either.

If you want more freedom, you must show that you understand the purpose of the rules, follow them regularly, and act responsibly. Your *inner-circle-adults* want to know that you can handle stress and temptations on your own because they will not always be there to guide you. Don't put yourself in situations that you are unprepared to handle. Ask for as much input as you need. If you bite off more than you can chew, don't worry. Your *inner-circle-adults* will stand with you because of your excellent history with them. Again, don't worry. Your history does not have to be perfect, but you need a good reputation for communicating, responding agreeably to correction, and doing the best you know how.

In any case, don't take anything for granted. Revisit the rules set by your parents and other adults in your life. Some intentional dialogue as discussed in chapter 5 might be needed if you find yourselves at an impasse. Realize that even adults have rules to follow, so if you don't like them at least learn not to resent them. Rules are not designed to make your life miserable. They are designed to keep you and others safe from harm.

When THEY Don't Know You

When you venture outside your circle of friends and adults, dealing with those in authority can be very stressful and dangerous. It is a world of unknown expectations for you and for those you encounter. Encounters that can be especially troubling are those involving police officers or a police action whether you have broken the law or not.

Get informed about what to expect and practice how you will react before it happens. That means you need to think ahead and plan your actions and responses to avoid negative interactions with the police. These are dangerous times, but everyone, the police, and all our citizens should still expect to be treated with respect. Unfortunately, getting respect is not automatic but is based on expectations that everyone involved may not understand the same way. So, be sure you know what to expect based on reality, not assumptions, or stories from others who may be stretching the truth or are otherwise uninformed.

We have heard the word "police" in many different contexts.

The "police" can be defined as the civil force of a national or local government, responsible for the prevention and detection of crime and the maintenance of public order. Then there is "police" as an action word. This action can be taken by an agent of the government or by you. You can and should police yourself first and foremost. Avoid placing yourself in a position that somebody else (namely the official police) must be summoned to a destination where you have participated in criminal conduct or disorderly behavior.

The police are called to help maintain order when there is disorder. When you decide to police yourself, you will maintain self-order by not acting in ways to draw negative attention to yourself or by breaking laws. There is a time and a place for all kinds of lawful behaviors but be aware of how your actions in different spaces at unexpected or unscheduled times may cause alarm to others.

Remember your rights end where it infringes or limits the rights of others. For example, you have a right to play music, but not if the volume is deemed unreasonably early in the morning or late at night. There are some statues or laws that set standards for what is considered unreasonable or unlawful in your area. Your neighbors may be disturbed and speak to you without calling the police. Take that opportunity to police yourself. You do have specific rights, but do not base the exercise of those rights on television shows, your friends' bad advice, or even your feelings. Instead, exercise your rights based on verified facts, knowledge of your surroundings, reasonable expectations for your behavior, cooperation with those in authority, and good common sense for your survival.

Whenever there is a time that you are forced into interactions with the police, take the initiative to police yourself by being compliant (doing what is instructed) and nonconfrontational. Follow all instructions that you are given in an orderly manner. When that happens, everyone involved has a better chance of walking away from the interaction unhurt because you have policed yourself.

After you have complied but believe that you have not been treated fairly or that your rights have been violated, immediately report that information to your parents or another responsible adult to help you file a formal complaint. If possible, write down the officer's name and badge number. Most importantly write down all the information surrounding those circumstances while it's fresh on your mind.

At the end of the day, the goal is that you, other members of the public, and police officers are not physically harmed nor emotionally traumatized.

Problems and Solutions

Suppose you find yourself in a new school or a new class with a teacher who does not know you, but you are surrounded by your buddies who expect certain antics from you. Peer pressure, ugh! It can be hard to resist but resist anyway.

Best Scenario at School: Follow the rules of the classroom. Introduce yourself to the teacher either before or after class, so they have a sense of who you are. Don't seek to be a celebrity student. (At least not right away!)

A Not-So-Good Scenario at School: You make an innocent joke, and your buddies laugh too loud and too long. Your last teacher knew you would never be disrespectful, that you are a great student and a leader she can depend on. But this new teacher does not know you and tries to make an example of you to show the class that disruptions will not be allowed.

What do you do? Take the public consequences and do what is asked of you. Later, talk with the teacher in private, apologize, and establish an understanding of what she or he can expect from you in the future.

> ***You can use similar responses to handle comparable scenarios when joining a sports team or on a new job.**

A lot of teachers are very conscientious about finding out about who is coming to their classrooms, so they will be ready for you. But remember teachers and other adults are people too with the daily pressures of life. Give them a break and you might get one in return. Every school district, college, and university has a student handbook that includes your rights and responsibilities. Be familiar with the general contents and refer to it if any need arises.

Let's Summarize

So, if they know you or they don't' know you

1. Make sure that you understand the rules and the consequences.

2. Follow the rules consistently even if you don't *feel* like it.

3. Promptly communicate anything that may interfere with you following the rules.

4. Watch your tone of voice and your body language. Both can betray you by revealing your fear, anger, or resentment, which could trigger negative reactions from those in authority.

5. Try to remain calm and not appear to be either offensive or defensive.

6. Realize all rules may not seem fair but exist for reasons that may not apply to you directly but to safeguard everyone.

7. Safeguard your own emotional and physical safety. Police yourself!

✏️ Teen assignment

Set your own standards. Consider these questions and write down your responses in your journal. How do you want to be treated by others? What do you believe is the best way to act to get a positive response from them? What attributes do you want others to see in you: trustworthy, sensible, well-mannered, reasonable, good natured, studious, creative, achiever, problem-solver, peacemaker, leader, etcetera ?

Choose the top three or four attributes that you want others to think of when you come to their mind.

Do you have it, or do you need it?

Attribute	Have it?	Need it?

Devise a plan to magnify the positive attributes you have and a plan to acquire those that you don't have. For instance, if you want to be known as an achiever, set an academic, personal, or community-based goal. As you devise steps to achieve it, ask for input from your teachers, like-minded students, parents/guardians, and members of your community.

Let them know of your progress and challenges along the way. Ask for their help when and if you need it. When you achieve that goal, they will all have been part of your process and BINGO! You are now known as an achiever!

💡 Parent-Teen Share

Try this role reversal activity.

You will play the authority figure and your parents will play the youth in trouble or in need of correction. If you have two parents, they can play all at once or take turns. Everyone can switch roles.

Some sample role-playing scenarios.

- You skipped school because a teacher made you mad.
- Your grades have gone down, and you have not been bringing any books home to study.
- Parents/guardians yell and ground your child for not cleaning their room.
- Parents/guardians demonstrate extreme disappointment and ground your child for not making all A's and B's.

Be sure to use the physical demeanor, the language and the tone of the role you are assuming. It's okay to exaggerate a bit to get your point across.

After you go through a scenario, discuss and journal your responses to these questions.

- How did it make you feel?
- Was the feeling of wearing someone else's shoes different than you thought it would be?
- Did the outcome of your scenario seem real or at least close to real?
- Did the other person get your reactions right for the most part?
- What do you think they got wrong?
- How can you, in your real-life role, help create a better outcome for both of you?

- What is your take -away about the importance and the role of authority?

For students/youth: Do you feel that authority is necessary? Will you feel comfortable if nothing was required of you? Do you believe that you will be successful in life without rules to live by?

Moral authority comes from following universal and timeless principles like honesty, integrity, and treating people with respect. —Stephen Covey

Journal Entry: Role- Reversal Exercise

_____

_____

_____

_____

_____

_____

_____

_____

_____

_____

_____

_____

_____

_____

_____

_____

_____

_____

_____

_____

_____

_____

Chapter 7

BE SMART: Social Media vs Real Talk

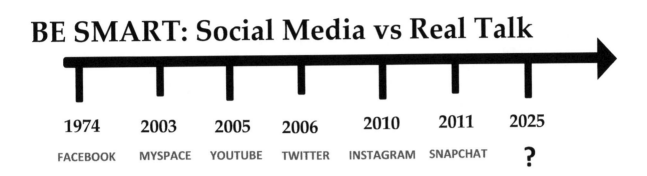

1974	2003	2005	2006	2010	2011	2025
FACEBOOK	MYSPACE	YOUTUBE	TWITTER	INSTAGRAM	SNAPCHAT	?

The Arrival of Social Media

A study released on January 22, 2018 shows there is a correlation between how much happiness teens feel and the time they spend online, including texting and social media use.[6]

Whether you are an introvert or extrovert, knowing how to be social is essential for your maturity. Unfortunately, today's teens and young adults have more to deal with than earlier generations when it comes to managing relationships with the growing demands to "share" on social media platforms. Facebook has been around since 1974, YouTube since 2005, and newer social media platforms like Snapchat and Instagram have emerged as the latest rage among teens. Eventually, new platforms will be developed, and pre-existing ones will be transformed for an expanding base of consumers. It is a trend that will most likely stay around for years to come. So, it's important to know how to handle social media, or it may handle you.

Is social media bad for your health?

Do your social media habits support current relationships or build new ones? Do they expand your opportunities to connect with friends, family, and the greater community? Or has it become a source of irritation, anxiety, or depression? You can make social media choices to expand your horizons instead of those that contribute to the misery of miscommunication that can lead to isolation. Many parents worry about how exposure to technology affects teens and young adults, both socially and developmentally. In fact, experts worry that social media and text messages that are such a big deal in the lives of teens and young adults, actually promote anxiety and lower self-esteem. A survey of 14 to 24-year-olds found that Snapchat, Facebook, Twitter, and Instagram all led to increased feelings of depression, anxiety, poor body image, and loneliness.[7] Strong evidence suggests that the over-exposure of social media has led to a mental health crisis among teens and young adults.

So how does this happen?

First, it begins with withdrawal from face-to-face contact. If you spend most of your social time online texting, sharing, trolling, and scrolling, you are putting yourself at risk. Virtual communication such as texting and messaging has its advantages, but it can also lead to miscommunication. Without real-time face-to-face contact, you are missing out on the benefits of critical social skills of real-time interactions which include tiny non-verbal social cues or social reactions such as body language, facial expressions, and slight changes in vocal quality.

You need to understand how an over-reliance on social media communication puts everybody at a disadvantage by wiping out the benefits of face-to-face interaction that are important to understand what one person could desperately be trying to express. Dr. Catherine Steiner-Adair, a clinical psychologist and author of *The Big Disconnect* argues that "there's no question kids are missing out on very critical social skills" when they overuse social media because as "a species we are very highly attuned to reading social cues."[8] This means we communicate best when we use all our senses which can only happen face-to-face.

Social media allows you to keep your guard up and create a false sense of who you are. This sense of emotional safety and self-invention can be enticing, but it can also be dangerous when reality catches up with you. Your social media presence should be a recognizable representation of who you are, which may include your best moments and a few challenges, but should never be anything too extreme that might come back to haunt you in the future. Don't expose personal issues that you would not want the entire world, friends, enemies, family, teachers, clergy, or potential employers to know about your life. Highly charged emotions are best shared off-line and face-to-face with a few trustworthy people. Once anything, pictures or text, goes on the Internet it can be found for all time, even if you delete it.

Social media has other risks: Cyberbullying and "Catfishing"

Staying plugged in means staying available for cruelty. This sense of safety from a distance has made it easier to be cruel. Bullies communicate all sorts of things that they would never say or do in a gazillion years to anyone's face.

Everyone on social media is at risk, but teenage girls and young women are especially vulnerable. As a group, they typically don't like to disagree with each other in "real life." Coach Lily

Of course, this is not true of all teenage girls or young adult women. Many times, the virtual world spills over into the real world with dire consequences such as physical assault and even suicide for teenage boys and young men, too.

Being a bully is not cool. In many cases, it is down-right criminal.

Doing the right thing

If this is you, or if this is any of your friends, there is something that you can do about it. Remember, that potentially, everyone is watching. Once you understand the pros and cons, you can make deliberate choices on the best ways to use social media, and when that form of communication is appropriate or inappropriate. For example, posting an invitation to a public event can be a great and appropriate use of social media, or even posting funny animal videos. But putting someone on blast about a personal issue is not. When people feel humiliated or disrespected, they may lash out in ways that will not be beneficial to themselves or others. The answer may be to communicate in real-time *without* a virtual audience, which may help to NOT blow issues out of proportion.

It takes courage to be honest about your feelings, to listen to what the other person has to say, and then to respond appropriately. Learning to effectively communicate face-to-face across difficult bridges fueled by accusations, mistrust, or other issues may seem scary at first, but it is essential to becoming a well-adjusted adult with a respected role in a community. You may even gain an unexpected bonus, as respectfully handled disagreements *have* led to long-lasting friendships.

It takes courage to love yourself as you are. Do not feel forced to create a persona or image that even your family wouldn't recognize. It is perfectly acceptable to project what you want in your life and to present your best self. However, if you want to try on an entirely "new" life or experience, write a dramatic short story, a novel, or create a film instead. Otherwise, you may get caught up in a horrific thriller that may be difficult to escape.

Problems and Solutions

You may need to practice your face-to-face conversation techniques.

- Are you bored and don't have friends who share your interests? Join or start a club at school. Ask a teacher who teaches a related course or have a related interest to help you with that process.

- Search for and join specialty groups on Facebook that meet in person. Be sure to let a responsible adult help you to evaluate the groups and only meet in populated public spaces like libraries. Try to take an adult and a classmate or sibling with you to the first meeting for support and feedback.

- If you are over 18, there may be other options. If you don't know what you like, want to expand your horizons, or meet new people, search for face-to-face groups through online platforms such as Meetup™. You can join groups that interest you. You can start your own, but they have a minimal fee for organizers.

- Ask your school, library or church if you can host an interest meeting for a charitable cause, civic objective, or a social purpose. This will allow you to meet other people who share your values.

- Check community events in local newspapers and other local media outlets. There are usually assorted topics covered in free or low-cost classes or seminars offered by departments of recreation, community colleges, corporations, nonprofits, or some small businesses.

After visiting or joining any group, make sure they fit your expectations. If they don't move on until you find a good fit.

Let's Summarize

1. Don't become overly dependent on social media for your social outlet.
2. Don't overshare on social media. Keep personal moments personal.
3. Count to 10 before ranting online. What goes on the Internet stays on the Internet. Even if you delete it, a permanent record can be uncovered.
4. Don't create profiles that can possibly lead to trouble. Realize that you can have friends who accept you as you truly are.
5. Look for and develop opportunities for face-to face interactions.
6. Look for more opportunities to have meaningful face-to-face conversations.
7. Be safe and act responsibly.

Teen Assignment

Visit local museums and tour your city like a tourist. Or become an explorer in your own backyard. Take interesting pictures of what is already there or try staging some shots that you or other viewers may like. Create titles for each one or ask your social media friends to chime in.

Note: You can use a camera of a phone without data service to take photos and with Wi-Fi you can email them to yourself to upload to social media sites.

Once you start your real-time life you will have more to share in your virtual one!

Parent/Teen Share

Establish some general rules for courtesy so that social media will not disrupt your family's communication and time together.

Greet each other without rushing to send those emails or publish posts.

1. Develop a contract for accountability.

Set limits on usage that both parents and teens will abide by. Establish technology-free zones and hours when no one uses the phone, including your parents or guardians. Set aside time to communicate with each other without your phone, tablet, or laptop on the ready. Take off that Bluetooth device during those times.

> *Mealtimes, a traditional family time, would be great, but there are times when various responsibilities do not allow for shared meals. A lot of families have very little time to spend together during the day, so they make use of early mornings and early evenings at home or during commutes to and from school and work.*

2. Get in a habit of sharing with each other.

Establish and maintain open communication about your social media use and the things that affect you, whether it's news about a catastrophe or an issue that a friend or family member shares on social media. There is so much information and attitudes represented on social media that may not represent your family's views. Be sure to ask questions and share your thoughts. Give each other a reality check about both significant and trivial things.

"No, dad, we don't have a problem with smoking at my school." 😦

"Yes, daughter, I know how to do the hustle." 😉

> *Sharing a funny video can be just as impactful to your relationship as a news story. Family members who laugh*

together are happier together. Shared humor creates bonds and establishes security.

3. **Commandeer social media to build family relationships.**
Create a closed or secret family group on a social media platform to share and collect recipes, family photos, updates on projects: family, school, or individual. Almost all social platforms have a group setting. Choose the one that is best for your purpose and make sure you understand the settings that ensure the level of privacy you want. By setting up a group, your family will be notified each time someone publishes a post. Remember it will be important to check in and respond regularly or it won't be social, right?☺

Don't waste words *on* people *who* deserve your silence. Sometimes *the* most powerful thing you can say *is* nothing *at* all. —*Mandy Hale*

6. "6 Takeaways from a Study about Teens' Happiness and Time Spent Online." Washington Post. 22 Jan 2018. <https://www.grandforksherald.com/lifestyle/4391753-6-takeaways-study-about-teens-happiness-and-time-spent-online>
7. *Instagram* 'Worst for young mental health.' 19 May 2017 <https://www.bbc.com/news/health-39955295>
8. Catherine Steiner-Ad. Teresa H. Barker. *The Big Disconnect: Protecting Childhood and Family Relationships in the Digital Age.* HarperCollins Publishers, NY 2013.

Chapter 8

Toxic People...Toxic Life

If you run around with cynical, negative people all the time, you will become cynical and negative. Unconsciously, you will pick up their ways and habits. -Les Brown[9]

Identifying Toxic People

Have you ever dealt with someone (or you may be dealing with someone right now) that just drains all your positive energy every time you interact with them? Has anyone made you feel so drained that when you leave them you feel you need to physically rest or just be by yourself to get your energy level up again?

These people are toxic because just like poison, they are harmful to your well-being. Toxic people may play various roles in your life such as friends, co-workers, family members, or occasional associates. They may seem to brighten your day only to drop you to the point of despair if you let them. They can drain the very energy out of you and bring out the worst in you! They seem to affect you the most when you have your guard down. They totally stress you out...physically, mentally and emotionally!

The main goal of a toxic person is to manipulate other people. They do that in numerous ways. One way is to make you feel inadequate. If you are always unsure of yourself when they are around, you may be dealing with a toxic person. Like gummy bears they have many flavors, but all of them drain your energy. You will never know which version of them will show up. They will be happy with you one day and the next day they will act like your worst enemy, then flip back again. You spend most of your time trying to make up for something you didn't do. You begin to wonder things like: "Am I a bad person?" "Am I stupid" "Did I misunderstand something?" You find yourself apologizing over and over again to win their acceptance. You even begin making excuses for their behavior. You start to believe that you did something to deserve this treatment. You feel you always have to defend yourself. If you are experiencing these symptoms on a continual basis with anyone in your life, it is not a healthy relationship, it's a toxic one.

So, what can you do? First, stop trying to please them. We often defend people in our head because we want to think the best of them. We hate to think that someone could be that way, but it is what it is. Stop making excuses for their bad behavior. Stop defending yourself to them. Do your best at any moment in time. That is all that you are required to do. You are a caring person who knows how to treat others. So, trust your gut. If you think you may have done something to hurt somebody, ask them, and talk about it. Apologize, if you did hurt them and move on. You shouldn't have to guess, and you shouldn't have to keep paying and paying with no end in sight.

Another way that toxic people try to manipulate others is to pretend that they are doing them a favor. They may often make you feel that you owe them something. For instance, they may say, "We can study at my house since it's closer, but you need to bring the snacks." Then all the while you're there they spend the time copying your notes. Or they play with your ego and your sympathy by saying things like, "You know that you'll be getting an A, but if I fail, I won't pass this class." Then they contribute nothing while benefitting from all your hard work of paying attention and taking notes. You don't owe them your work. They had the same opportunity but chose to do something else instead. Remember to think before you act: Is this manipulation or is this a favor for someone in real need? Is it fair to you or does it hurt others? Are they abusing your friendship? Does it provide a benefit they have not earned? Would they do the same for you? If it doesn't feel like a favor, it's probably not.

A third way they like to manipulate is to project their feelings on you. If they are angry with you, they may say, "You've been acting funny lately. Are you mad with me?" In reality, your toxic companions are mad with you, but by saying that, they make you squirm. Then you try to convince them that you haven't been acting *funny*. In doing so, you find yourself apologizing your way back into their good graces and doing favors you may not have normally committed yourself to do. Afterall, you made *them* feel bad.

So how do you know if you are dealing with a toxic person?

- Do they lie and cheat on a regular basis? (If the answer is yes. They could be toxic.)
- Do they ever apologize when they are wrong? (If the answer is no. They could be toxic.)
- Do they give you the silent treatment? (If the answer is yes. They could be toxic.)
- Can you trust them with your feelings? (If the answer is no. They could be toxic.)
- Are you constantly apologizing due to their over-sensitivity? (If the answer is yes. They could be toxic.)
- Are they judgmental and make you feel guilty most of the time? (If the answer is yes. They could be toxic.)

The whole agenda of toxic people is to control your emotions and your actions through manipulation. When they learn to push your emotional buttons, they will play you like a piano. During your whole life, you will be faced with demanding and stressful situations in all areas of your life: personal, school or work-related. Stay focused and choose a sound path based on self-affirming principles to overcome these challenges as they arise.

Self-affirming principles allow you to maintain your self-worth and self-esteem.

Keep a positive attitude and respect yourself enough to walk away from anything and anyone that causes you to be anxious and stressed. Some people can't be pleased, and some people won't be good for you – and many times that will have nothing to do with you. You can always say "no" to unnecessary foolishness.

Be confident. Own your own faults, your quirks as well as the things that make you shine. You don't need anyone's approval but remember if someone is working hard to manipulate, it's probably because they want *your* approval. That's okay, to a point. However, you are not obligated to give it, but if you do, don't let the cost be too high. No matter the outcome, protect yourself, and make the best decisions you can.

What will your life be like without toxic people?

You are going to have so much more peace in your life. You are going to be so much more positive. Your creative thoughts and ideas will flow so much more freely. You deserve to be happy and the normal activities of life are stressful enough. You need to spend your time learning, growing in wisdom, becoming the best you, and not being hindered by toxic people.

📎 Problems and Solutions

Problem 1: You have toxic people in your family or other close relationships that you cannot avoid.

Solution: Set boundaries. You teach people how to treat you by how you respond to them. Avoid responding out of anger, which could get you in hot water if you don't think things through before acting or speaking. What do you need to happen? How can you respond respectfully, but maintain your sense of self? How can you stop being manipulated? Set boundaries, which are the lines you draw that teach people how far they can go before you speak up or stop them. If you do not draw any boundaries, they will push you to your limits and beyond.

For example, you know your sibling always sticks you with the dishes because out-of-the-blue they have a project due or a social function they must attend. You don't want them to get in trouble, do you? You don't want their social life to be ruined, do you? Yeah, right! The guilt trip is a go-to manipulation trick for toxic people. Tell them, "No" before it happens. Put them on notice and stick to it. Let them know that you will not continue to take up the slack for them. It's great to be helpful, but toxic people take advantage on a regular basis and never return the favor.

Toxic people, even our loved ones, usually do not change without a fight. So be prepared for being ignored, overlooked, getting the silent treatment, or worse.[10] Whatever the price, it will be worth it because you will be free.

Problem 2: Sometimes, we are the toxic ones. Here are some signs:

Signs that you are toxic!

- You have a lot of friends and family distancing themselves from you.
- People seem unhappy to be around you.
- You always feel like a victim and tell that to anyone who will listen.
- You must be in control of everything that happens.
- You find yourself saying cruel things to other people.
- You need to be validated by other people to feel good about yourself.
- You have an addiction problem.
- You are constantly thinking negative thoughts about yourself and your life.

- You take everything very personally and find ways to make other people pay for it.
- You gossip about others and put them down.[10]

Solution: If you see these behaviors in yourself, then you may be the problem. Admit it. You may feel angry, upset, drained, or mistreated by other people, but that may simply be because you are a toxic person who has a very negative viewpoint of other people.

Total honesty will help you feel much better about yourself and your family. If you can take the time to get honest about your toxic contribution to other people's lives, you will take the time to find ways to fix it. When that happens, you may find that all your relationships will suddenly become much more loving, energizing, and rewarding. Go out of your way to show that you are aware of your actions and make a sincere gesture that you are working on it. Stay the course, ask for constructive feedback as needed. Beating yourself up about the past is a waste of time. Make amends when possible. Most importantly, start making the changes that you need for a better future, a future in which people love to see you coming instead of leaving.

Let's Summarize

Number 1: Learn to identify toxic people by the way they interact with you and the way they make you feel. Trust your intuition.

Number 2: Defeat their effect with toxic-busting strategies of realizing your worth and blocking negative influences on your emotions with thoughts and activities that make you feel good about yourself and your life.

Number 3: Check yourself for toxicity. Change your mindset and your actions as needed.

Number 4: Make decisions that will create a happier, more successful, toxic-free life.

✏ Teen Assignment

Get rid of toxic people!

Explore your tools and settings for privacy to use limiting and blocking tools on your phone, email accounts, and on social media. Don't let toxic talk or images enter your social media accounts. If people insist on creating or sending responses that you feel are negative or offensive, do not join in to become part of "the crowd." Follow your own standards. In the end, this will allow you to connect with more like-minded people.

Limit your face-to-face interactions with toxic people. Limit their access to you. If you cannot avoid them, make a plan to deal with them. Set boundaries and stick with them. If they refuse to let you have peace, do not take their calls, texts, email or social media communication, ever!

Create affirmations to fight the specific negativity that toxic people place in your mind that may be limiting you or making you feel bad about yourself. For example, they may have planted the seed, "You are always late!" Your affirmations to combat it may be something like the following:

I am becoming more and more efficient with my time.
I am always in control of how I manage my time.
I always know what I am supposed to be doing.
I am on time, all the way!

🔆 Parent-Teen Share

Set aside a time for a "how-are-you-doing" check-up. This can be a quick daily exchange and you can set aside time every week for a table talk with your favorite beverage in your favorite spot. Write notes to each other during the week to start conversations for when you get together. When you meet, be sure to end on a positive note. Some issues cannot be settled at once, but you can develop a plan of action and follow up to see how it's going.

Especially for Parents: Remember that your children are not you, so don't question whether they should or should not be having a particular problem. Listen more than you talk. Focus more on asking questions that will allow your teen to come up with their own solutions instead of offering solutions that may not be as realistic for them as you may think. Try seeing things from their perspective. Give them emotional support and help them think through how to set proper boundaries but allow them to handle it themselves as much as possible. Stand ready to do more only if it becomes necessary.

"When you say 'yes' to others, make sure you are not saying 'no' to yourself. — Paulo Coelho

---

9. Les Brown, called "The Motivator," is a world renown motivational speaker and author of many books including "15 Minutes a Day to Manifest the Life of Your Dreams."
10. "10 Signs You Have Toxic Family Members And 3 Things You Can Do About It." *Mercury*, 2 Dec. 2015

Chapter 9

Your Inner Circle

> The Law of the Inner Circle:
> A leader's potential is determined by those closest to him.
> ~ John C. Maxwell

The term "inner circle" is a way to describe all the people that are closest to you emotionally and psychologically. You depend on them and they depend on you for support, purpose, and oftentimes for socializing or entertainment activities. Together you celebrate good times and you help each other through troubled times. You inspire each other and have strong bonds built on trust and the knowledge of each other's hearts and minds. You laugh together, cry together, dream together, and make plans together. These are the people who you hang out with. They are the people who will have the biggest influence in your life!

The old saying that "birds of a feather, flock together" is true. Who you spend your time with will greatly influence every area of your life. They will have a mighty influence on your beliefs, your attitude, your actions, and your success. Knowing this, don't you want people in your inner circle that will add value to you?

Of course, you do, and the good news is that you have total control of who is allowed within your inner circle! There may be many things that are not in your control but the one thing you have absolute control over is your circle of influence. Throughout your life, you get to choose your associates, confidants, friends, and mentors. So, you get to decide who can influence what you aim for and whether you will succeed. Determine who you want to be, what you want to represent, and choose your inner circle accordingly. There are guidelines for making wise decisions on how to choose those persons in your inner circle. Ask yourself these questions about each member of your inner circle!

Questions	Yes	No
Does he or she add value to me? (Am I better with them than without them?)		
Do they help me to be the best me that I can be? (Do they inspire me to do my best?)		
Are they respectful to me and others? (Are they polite and courteous?)		
Are they respected by our peers, teachers, and other adults? (Do others speak highly of them?)		
Do they have integrity? (Do they do what is right even when no one in authority is watching them?)		
Do they encourage me to act responsibly? (Are they examples of good behavior?)		
Am I constantly in trouble when I associate with them? (Do I have to apologize for my behavior?)		
Have they *earned* a bad reputation? (Do people hate to see them coming?)		

Two other important questions that you may need to ask when considering who to allow in your inner circle are: "Do they positively impact others in my circle? Do they make others in my circle better? Remember, your circle of influence are those closest to you, so you should feel a strong sense of responsibility towards each other.

But I don't want to be stuck up!

Choosing your inner circle is not being "stuck-up" or snobbish. However, only choosing people based on your proximity to them or those in your neighborhood may not be the best way to decide, either. Some judgment is necessary. Members of your inner circle do not have to be just like you in every way. Differences can be a great asset, but you should enhance each other's lives in significant ways. Valuing, respecting and acknowledging differences in culture, backgrounds, and identities will increase your ability to live more successfully as an adult. So, don't exclude anyone based on insignificant differences. The most important thing is to choose people who share your core values such as trustworthiness, honesty, loyalty, sense of humor, or whatever characteristics that will add value to your life and are valuable to you in a friend. Develop your own must-have list. You may discover someone with a gift that you may not have any other way of experiencing who can add significant meaning to your life. Learning to be tolerant, accepting, and even loving of those who may seem different than you will teach you more about the world. Be approachable when possible. There are many great people in the world; however, beware! Everybody cannot be in your inner circle. Show yourself to be friendly, helpful, and compassionate, but don't make the mistake of letting someone into your inner circle who does not share your core values. So, the membership into your inner circle may be small. The members may live near or far. It's your life, so it's up to you to make the best of it by not leaving your inner circle to chance.

So, Your Best Friend "Ghosted" You?

There may come a time when someone who you thought was a friend, maybe even a best friend, will decide to disappear from your life. You may never hear about it directly from them, but it could happen slowly or all at once. It stings, and the fact you didn't see it coming makes it even worst. But were there signs? Have their interests and goals changed? Have yours? Did a specific occurrence happen that you can pinpoint as a moment that changed everything, a moment that you felt uncomfortable or one that made them feel uncomfortable? Did you or they violate or do something against the "friend code" without knowing it? Did you or they violate a sacred trust and thought it was no big deal? Oftentimes guilt can drive a wedge between people. There is a good possibility that neither of you has done anything wrong at all. You could have just started down different paths and simply moved on before you realized it. People can simply grow apart. The good news is that you may rediscover each other later in life. Either way, be thankful for the good times you did have. Do not trash their name or tell their secrets. If you do, you may risk losing the trust of the new friends that will come your way. Be a person of integrity.

Yes, it may feel like any other break-up. You may wonder, " Who are they hanging out with now?" You may be angry at them and all their new friends. You may have bouts of anger but do not act on them. You may experience extreme sadness and cry. Let it pass through you but don't let it linger. You will get past it. You may never know the "whys" of the break-up. So, try not to let it take over your daily thoughts. Acting out on these feelings can be counterproductive to your life. Instead, fill the void with something productive like pursuing new interests with those who may become new friends. You will find other friends but let all your friendships develop naturally. If you are a good friend, you will attract others who will appreciate your qualities.

As you grow older, you will find your tribe, a group of devoted friends who will be there for you in good and in challenging times. These friends will value who you are, not require you to be a carbon-copy of them or want you for one-way favors.

Close, long-lasting friendships are important for your development.

Your tribe will sustain you during tough times. Finding the right people for your tribe usually takes years to accomplish, but don't worry about it. You will have that special friend again. Just keep being true to yourself and you will find each other. Members of your inner circle may change as all of you mature and get to know yourselves better, but some may endure until the end.

Let's Summarize

Evaluate your inner circle by the values that you hold for yourself. Some associations will come to an end because people change. Are they still being just as good a friend as you are to them? Are you proud or happy about your association with them on any level? Over time, some members of your inner circle may begin to be more trouble and aggravation than justifies your continued association. Being a great friend who can be depended on to listen or to make you feel better when you need it can be of immense value. However, walk away from people who are not adding any value to your life. The sooner you learn to make these changes, the more control you will have over your life. These will be lifelong consequences because your inner circle will have the most significant effect on your attitudes, decisions, and overall success of your life. Keep your inner circle, tight!

⌗ Problems and Solutions

Problem: Betrayal by a former member of your Inner Circle and the resulting rumor mill.

Tony and you had been great friends since third grade. You shared everything with him. You walked to school together, ate at each other's homes, had sleepovers and played sports together. He was your buddy for life, so you thought. As you grew older, you grew taller, broader, and became even more athletic. Making friends was easy for you. You were popular with the cool kids and the so-called nerds. Tony, however, stopped growing in height about three years ago. This made a difference in his attitude toward you, but you didn't notice. He is your friend. Nothing can change that, right? Although Tony was still pretty good at sports, your abilities surpassed his by leaps and bounds. So, Tony turned his attention to science and won many awards for his projects. You do okay, but Tony really has a knack for science. You are still friends and hang out occasionally, but you both are busier with your different activities. Just as you become known as a formidable athlete, Tony is known as a formidable opponent when it comes to anything science related. One day, Tony sees you talking to his lab partner, a pretty, popular girl named Mindy. You are both all smiles and leaning in as if conjuring up a conspiracy. Tony's been meaning to ask Mindy for a date, but he hadn't gotten his nerve up yet. He gets jealous looking at the two of you together. (Little does he knows, that both of you were talking about him and marveling over how smart he is.) Later that evening, to knock you down a peg in Mindy's eyes, Tony shares an embarrassing but true story with her. He tells Mindy about that time you stole money from your mother's purse to buy a video game. Of course, Tony doesn't mention that it was on a dare or that it was 5 years ago. Nor does he tell her how sorry you were or that you confessed and made it right with your mother that same day. The most significant thing that he did not tell Mindy is that you shared that story to keep him from making a similar mistake. However, Mindy repeats the story to you (and maybe a few others).

Solution: Don't feel that you must deny it or confirm it. Most importantly, do not withdraw from the world. Talk about it with someone you can trust and has no interest in passing the story along, such as a parent/guardian, counselor, or a trusted older friend to relieve the pressure. They can probably give you a better perspective. Realize that you do not owe your classmates an explanation. Just shrug it off and remind them of who you are now. Your real friends know you and will stand by you.

In most cases, starting a campaign of denial will make the "story" hang around longer. If the rumors get out of hand and begin to harm your other relationships or your academic performance, immediately seek help from your parents. Your school counselor or other licensed professional may also need to get involved. Harassment and bullying are never acceptable. Make no mistake about it, serious repercussions are often the outcome of telling other peoples' secrets.

Your friendship with someone who betrays your secrets may be irreparable. Mourn the loss of the trust you once shared and forgive them when you can. The sooner you do, the sooner you will be free of the matter. Confronting them may be useless. They will more than likely not tell you the real reason they did it nor will they be sorry. If they are, they may come to you... eventually. But maybe not. In any case, it will haunt them long after you have moved on.

Most importantly, do not condemn yourself for your past actions or for trusting someone. We can't always know what others will do. Hopefully, the betrayer will learn from their mistake but even if they don't, you will. Realize that whatever "the story" is, it was the story of a past version of yourself, one who has become wiser and more disciplined. As far as the rumor mill, people will find another topic eventually. Draw a line in the sand between the past and the present then move ahead.

Teen Assignment

Inner Circle Map

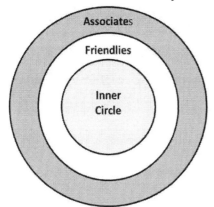

Create Your Inner Circle Map

Look at the *sample* to the left to draw your Inner Circle Map. Who is in your **Inner Circle**? They understand your humor or at least put up with it. They miss you when you aren't around and come looking for you to make sure you are okay.

Who are your **Friendlies**? These are people that you may speak to regularly and may hang with, if no one from your Inner Circle is around.

Your **Associates** are people that you know in passing. You usually interact with them when you want to achieve specific tasks that they can help you with and vice versa. Consider why each person is in each section of your map. Are they in the right circle? Fill in your personal associations circle below.

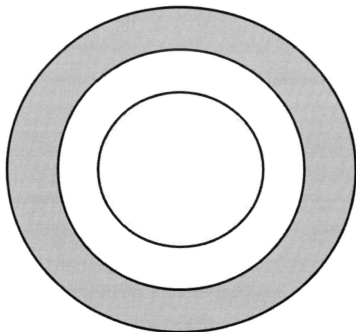

Identify Your Top 5

"Ride and Live" Success Buddies

Inner Circle Top 5	Describe their personality, skills, attitude, experience, etc.
Jim	Easy to get along with. Great at fixing electronics. Has patience and get along well with adults. Makes good grades.

If you have less than five, that's great! Be selective.

It's about quality not quantity.

Our inner circle do not have to be exactly like us, but they should complement or add something to our lives. In your journal or in the space below, **complete the title and recall a story** when your similarities or differences with one or more members of your group led to a positive outcome such as helped you overcome a problem or achieve a goal.

The Inside Scoop: _____

_____

_____

_____

_____

_____

_____

_____

_____

_____

_____

_____

_____

_____

_____

_____

_____

_____

_____

Parent-Teen Share

Activity 1: Connecting Activities

1. Create opportunities to build your special Inner Circle relationship with each other. At first, choose activities that can be completed within a brief time frame and that don't require a long-term commitment. Make sure all involved wants to continue them or move on to something different.

   - Volunteer together. Find something you both can contribute to in a significant way. This should not be a tag along project for either of you.
   - Attend a free concert that you both will enjoy
   - Choose a meal and cook it together
   - Plan a movie night at home
   - Take a short-term art class together
   - Build something together
   - Co-host a board game night for family and friends

Activity 2: Best Friend Story Swap

Share a *story* about a friend in your Inner circle. The twist is to choose a well-known story or re-read a picture-book by inserting that person into the story. Include details to reveal their personality traits, the ones you like and the ones you may find annoying. Go ahead, exaggerate a bit to make your *new* story interesting, amusing, or to make a point. Enjoy this time together. You can use this activity to begin difficult conversations. By sharing your stories, you may learn more about each other, become more empathetic, and much more.

Chapter 10

Watch Your Words: Think First

> Be careful with your words. Once they are said,
> they can be only forgiven, not forgotten." ~Unknown

WORDS CAN HURT

When I was growing up, parents armed their children with the saying, "Sticks and stones may break my bones, but words will never hurt me." The purpose of this children's rhyme was to prepare us and protect us from one of the harsh realities of life…words can hurt. I have even taught my children the same rhyme to help them ignore negative words used to hurt them in one way or another. A wise person once said that "people remember the positive things you say for two days, but they remember the negative things you say for six." The numbers of days may not be exact, but science has proven that negative memories impact us much longer than positive ones. Psychologist Patricia Evans, warns that "words can be as damaging to the mind as physical blows are to the body," and "the scars from verbal assaults can last for years."[11] Repeatedly dishing out negative words to hurt, shame, or punish someone can be verbal abuse.

Have you been disrespecting or dishonoring someone with your words? There have been times, I have said something only to regret it later. Sometimes it was out of anger, out of ignorance, a lack of knowledge or it was due to a lack of understanding. As I've grown more mature, I'm grateful that new instances of regret have lessened. Most of these instances happened when I was a teen and young adult. I wish someone had shared with me what I am sharing with you about the power of words and I could have been spared those regrets of my youth. If your words do not uplift people, bring clarity to a situation, or add value to the conversation, just don't say it! If you give respect, you will most likely get respect. This goes for parents, teachers, and other adults as well as your peers. Even those much younger than you deserve respect.

Some young adults think that it's cool to trash-talk those in authority and those they want to impress or dominate. But you will not get positive results with that behavior. This kind of negative communication can lead to present and future failures. You may need assistance to accomplish a goal or feel secure within your environment. Others, even adults, may not offer you the help or security you need unless it is absolutely required of them. Demonstrating respect by using positive words are keys to goodwill. People work harder to help people who make them feel good about helping them. That's a fact of life. Make a good impression with positive words instead of a bad impression with negative ones.

You need to let your words represent you well everywhere you go and in all areas of your life. This includes your home, school, sporting events, work, places of worship, and everywhere in your community with both your peers and adults. Words you speak in private may find their way into public spaces. You especially need to avoid harsh words and profanity on all social media outlets because those words will be around for as long as the Internet exists. Even if you delete every hateful, angry word, they can still be discovered by those who have the specific skills to do so. A lot of people have those skills, and that number is growing. This is not meant to scare you. It is to help you understand the far-reaching power of your words. If you have gotten caught up in the past, don't fret but stop the behavior at once. Never do trash talk online again. If you feel the need to vent, write it on paper or share it in a safe environment with a trusted few after you have cooled down and had time to process your anger. Always be more willing to listen than to speak. Remember once you let those words out of your mouth or on social media, you cannot push them back in! No one is perfect, but we are judged by our pattern of behavior. If your pattern of negative trash-talking ends, that will speak volumes in your favor.

Don't let negative words get the best of you. If you find yourself being badmouthed or bullied, don't give their words the power to change how you feel about yourself. Don't let your response mirror their unruly behavior. Silence is golden and will often shut down their attacks when they realize that you are not responding to their bad behavior. Continue to speak words of peace and words that inspire, praise and encourage those around you. Kind words are music to our ears, even to a bully.

What if the negative communication escalates? Notify your parents, administrators, or other supervising adults who are charged with the responsibility of keeping you safe from abuse. Verbal and online abuse are just as bad as physical abuse and may be an illegal act of harassment. Review the policy of your school, your place of employment, or other organization that connects you to the abuser. If threats are being communicated, you may need to go to the police. Follow the steps set by your school and your parents. You should not have to suffer from harassment and verbal abuse.

WORDS CAN BUILD BRIDGES

Let me tell you a true story about a friend of mine who went to London as part of her college studies in a study-abroad program.

During some time off from her studies, she joined a couple of classmates for a weekend in Paris, France. She recognized a few written phrases in French and spoke even fewer. However, Paris was a dream destination for her. Upon her arrival, she made a point of making polite conversation with the manager of the flat they chose for their stay. Between her little knowledge of French and his knowledge of English, she expressed her admiration for France and how well she had been treated since she had been there. As it worked out, she was separated from her classmates and was forced to spend the day touring alone. This turned out to her advantage because while on her own, she was able to have the experience she really wanted. But then it came time for her to make her way back to London for her scheduled class meeting. As she checked out, the manager sensed her distress and offered to help her find her way to the train station. He took her suitcase in hand and walked four blocks to make sure that she was safely on the right train before leaving her to go about her journey. That trip turned out to be the highlight of her travel abroad that year. Now, suppose she had not made a point to speak kindly of French hospitality. Suppose, she chose instead to use offensive words like the "ugly American" stereotype that does not value other cultures. If she had not built a bridge of respect, instead of being safer and feeling empowered by an adventure, she would have been in despair, and her trip could have been a disaster.

Use words that can build bridges between you and those you know as well as those you don't.

Your words can change the opinion of someone who has a negative preconceived notion of who you are based on false representations or an unearned reputation. Speak truthfully and with kindness toward others. Remember to use your kind words before you need them. They will serve you well.

WORDS CAN CREATE SUCCESS

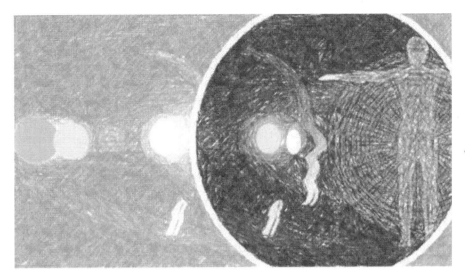

"Gentlemen, we can rebuild him.

We have the technology. We have the capability to make the world's first bionic man. Steve Austin will be that man."

"The Bionic Man"

These lines were the introduction to the hit television show, The Bionic Man (1974 to 1978), which led to a spinoff, The Bionic Woman (1976 to 1978). It may be a challenge to retrain or reprogram your thinking to say words that can create the life you want, but you can do it. Just as the TV scientists trusted that they could rebuild Steve Austin, similarly, you should trust that you can rebuild your life. Science has now proven that what we say can have real and measurable impact on our lives. So, you do have the power, the technology of your mind and your voice to rebuild your life to become who you want to be and live your best life.

Positive words can indeed train or retrain your brain for greater success [12]. But you must stop sabotaging yourself by repeating the same things you have heard from your environment that is now stuck in your head. Some of those negative phrases may be:

- "I'll always fail because I'm just not good at math."
- "I don't know how to make friends."

- ⚑ "I will never go to college or have a career that I love."
- ⚑ "I'll never be successful like those *people*."
- ⚑ *"I can never _____." You fill in the blank.*

Snap out of it! Stop speaking negative words about yourself. Speak words that will add value to your life. Give yourself the same advice you'd give to a trusted friend. Ask yourself the question, "If someone said this to me, how would it make me feel?" If good or great is not the answer, delete it from your brain and your speech. Your words can shape your reality. So, how does that work? If you say you will do something, you will take the steps to get it done. You will create a connection between your thoughts and your actions. But don't be afraid to ask for help to achieve your goals. No person succeeds alone. It will still be your success. Why be negative when you can choose to be positive?

⊖ COUNTERFEIT TRUTHS	⊕ REALISTIC TRUTHS
"I'll always fail because I'm just not good at math."	With some help, I will pass my math class.
"I don't know how to make friends."	I will be my best self, which is a friend.
"I will never go to college or have a career that I love."	I will have a happy life doing what I love. I can go to college and discover what that may be.
"I'll never be successful like those *people*."	I can create the lifestyle that will make me happy.
"I can never _____."	I can _____ with the right strategies and some help as needed.

Before long, you will be saying, "I'm winning at math! I have great friends! I'm excited about the career path for my future! I'm on schedule toward my success! I can do whatever I work to accomplish!

Let's Summarize

It is my hope that once you understand the true power of words, you will begin to speak positive things even if you don't see the results right away. When we know better, we should do better. Now, that I know how powerful words are, my conversation has changed and now yours should too! In most cases, if you can't say anything good, you should consider not saying anything at all!

Teen Assignment

1. **Let's go back to a standard: Write it out!** Putting your feelings on paper is an effective way to unload and identify the thoughts and behaviors you want to change.

Keep your journal right beside your bed, so you can start the positive transformation as soon as you are awake.

Take this practice beyond the written page and voice the positive change you want aloud. Don't say, "I am not going to get a bad grade in history." Instead proclaim, "I will pay attention in class, take notes, ask questions, and study to get a good grade in history." You may want to add, "I am a sponge for knowledge and will be successful in all my classes.

Other positive statements you may want to include in your morning routine are:

- ♥ *I choose peace.*
- ♥ *I am enough.*
- ♥ *I will always do my best.*

Rewrite History. Think about an incident that you felt you were at a loss for the right words to say. Imagine having a second chance or a do-over. What would you like to have said that may have changed the outcome? Realistically, we rarely have do-overs, but you can plan what to say in the future to make things turn out better if you ever have a similar encounter. It's better to have a well-thought-out response than to communicate a hurtful or harmful message. For instance, if someone asks you, "Do these pants make me look fat?" As an alternative to saying yes or no, choose to be truly helpful. According to Psychologist Susan Albers, you may practice saying something that addresses the underlying issue by reframing the question[11] and putting it back in their hands by asking, "How do you feel in that outfit?" Or, "What's really wrong?" By shutting down the self-shaming, you can help someone get in touch with what is really bothering them. We don't always know the best way to answer, so practicing is smart because practice makes us better. Eventually, more helpful responses will become more natural.

 Parent-Teen Share

Radio Show Game: "Can you be nice?!"

The Set-up: Each participant will create 6 questions to ask each other for a radio or TV show format. You may take no more than 5 minutes to pre-interview each other before the game begins. You should already be somewhat familiar with each other, right?

The Rules of Engagement: You can set the amount of points needed to win the game. I suggest that you start with 5 questions for a possible 5 points for each player. But it all depends on how long you want to play. You will take turns playing the Guest and the Interviewer. Only the Guest can win points. The Guest can win points by giving acceptable positive responses or if the Interviewer violates the rules by making a negative statement.

The Interviewer should ask questions about something that they believe the Guest will have difficulty answering with a positive response. (The Interviewer can get outside help with this.) As the Guest, you **cannot** say anything negative such as, "I don't like…" I hate…" or "I have a problem with…"

The Interviewer **cannot** respond with a negative statement or anything that outright contradicts the guest's responses.

For example, the Interviewer may ask, "What if broccoli was the only food in the house and you had to eat it?

> The Guest (who hates broccoli) responds, " You know I hate broccoli and would rather starve." Wrong! Disqualified!

> The Guest (who hates broccoli) responds, "I would be happy to eat anything that will keep me alive, since so many people don't have any food at all." A Correct Response! Score a point!

> If the Interviewer responds, "You know you'd rather die than eat broccoli!" Wrong! Guest gains a point.

> The Interviewer should nod approvingly or praise the Guest for their great response. A Correct Response! No additional points for the Guest.

Think of all the questions the Interviewer (teen or parent) can ask to make their Guests squirm while trying to protect their positive image! ♥

It's all for fun and learning, so don't get mad if things aren't going your way. Just by sharing, practicing positivity, and participating, everyone's a winner!

As the "Talk Show Host," or Interviewer, remember that your treasured guests have the power to crash your ratings leaving you without a job.

If you are the "Guest" being interviewed, you don't want to ruin your reputation, disappoint your fans, or lose the starring role that you have been offered, if this interview goes well. You both have millions of dollars at stake!

Some winning strategies for the "Can you be nice?!" game

- Be honest with your interactions but avoid criticizing anything!
- Use humor to cover small missteps against the rules.
- Try to create a win-win situation when possible but wait for the other player to slip up.
- Remember intentional silence can be golden. Let them sweat.
- Keep in mind that you will switch roles so both of you have something to gain and something to lose.

It is best if you have an audience to judge how you perform, but you can keep score with a mini chalkboard or with pen and paper.

Go for the win-win

It's not me or you, it's both of us. —*Sean Covey*

11. Albers, Susan. "'Does This Make Me Look Fat?' The Best Way to Respond." *Psychology Today*, Sussex Publishers, 22 Feb. 2011, www.psychologytoday.com/us/blog/comfort- cravings/201102/does-make-me-look-fat-the-best-way-respond.
12. Holland, Emily. "Retrain Your Brain: How to Reverse Negative Thinking Patterns." *The Chopra Center*, The Chopra Center, 8 Aug. 2018, chopra.com/articles/retrain-your-brain-how-to-reverse-negative-thinking-patterns.

Chapter 11
Healthy Body + Sound Mind
= Successful Life

Some good news!

With proper nutrition, exercise, and supportive adults in your life, most youth can have it all! That means you! A healthy diet and exercise are both necessary to have a healthy body. If you feel good physically, chances are that you will feel good mentally. There are a lot of terrific books on nutrition. All of them reveal that the basis of proper nutrition is eating a varied diet, with plenty of protein, green leafy vegetables, and liquids. Most suggest that your diet should be adjusted based on the level of your activity.

As far as maintaining a healthy mind, surrounding yourself by positive people, being grateful, and not letting yourself get pulled into other people's negative drama can go a long way. Most importantly, learning to recognize and deal with stress can be one of the most important skills you can master.

Even if you fall short in some areas, some of the time, you have the resilience of youth on your side to overcome the shortfalls of life. Seek knowledge from books, experts, and concerned adults to help you make the best choices. You have the power to overcome any odds if you believe in yourself. You can build a successful life!

What do the Experts say?

If you ask experts from various backgrounds on what being human means, you will get many different answers. However, there are two aspects of being human that everyone can agree on: humans thrive with good health and a sound mind. Good health and a sound mind are vital to our general well-being. Both enable us to gain the treasures of life. Some treasures are tangible which means they are available to our five senses of sight, touch, smell, hearing, and taste. When you place too much emphasis on insignificant tangibles, you can be easily manipulated. Your happiness and success will rest on shaky ground. Insignificant tangibles may satisfy you for a while, but over time the value they give to your life will be lost. Some treasures are intangible or cannot be experienced through our five senses, such as feelings of competence, self-reliance, accomplishment, responsibility, and self-respect. If you concentrate on building these treasures, you will always have something that cannot be lost or taken from you. To achieve the good things in life, you need to balance your life with a healthy body AND a healthy mind. It is important that you make wise decisions and take appropriate actions to manage and maintain your health in both areas of your life.

Preventable Threats to Your Healthy Body

According to the Center for Disease Control (CDC), the leading health-related problems in the ages 10-19 are early pregnancy, HIV, injuries including self-injury, tobacco use, and alcohol or drug-related diseases.[13] Most of these threats are due to risky behaviors. Behaviors are those things that you can control. Your health as a teen and young adult is mostly in your hands. Not only that, the choices you make now can affect your health for the rest of your life. I have heard the foolish brag, "I've got to die of something!" But the truth is that when young people contract many of these avoidable diseases, they could have an agonizing existence trying to manage them, to live, be happy, and be in some comfort for decades.

Don't fall into the trap of thinking your behaviors won't have consequences that you may have to deal with for the rest of a very long life that you may want to live for the future. Hopefully, medical science will alleviate many of these diseases in the future. Thankfully, there are now many therapies that can help reduce some of the discomforts of many conditions that will enable many to live longer and more comfortably. But why go down that road? Don't make decisions and take actions that can negatively affect your life forever! Choose to live a good life.

A Common Threat to Your Sound Mind: Depression

What is depression? Do I have depression?
What can be done about depression?

Depression is not feeling sad because something bad has happened or you because you saw a sad movie. It's not a feeling that can be waved away by eating ice cream or going to a party. It's a serious mood disorder that can change the way you think and function in your daily life. Depression can make you feel so tired that you can barely move. You have no energy and don't care about anything anymore.

As a result, you may begin having problems at home, at school, and in all areas of your life. Depression can hover like a dark cloud over every experience and every moment when it is upon you. You may feel hopeless and isolated, and it can seem like no one understands. You may want to go out with your friends because part of you don't want to be left behind, but your body refuses to make an effort to get ready, so instead you stay behind to nurse that dead feeling. Managing depression on your own is hard and feels almost unbearable. If you ever find yourself in this state of mind, please know that you are not crazy. Your depression is not a sign of weakness or a character flaw. However, you may need help.

☹ Depression is a serious illness that requires medical attention.

Depression is a medical condition that is far more common in teens and young adults than you may think. The hormonal changes, social challenges, and academic pressures, all contribute. Some of you may experience abuse from without and even from within your inner circles. This multiplies the problem. If you ever feel "blue" over extended periods, without any relief, you may be suffering from clinical depression.[13-2] This is not something you can just shake off. You need help. If this is your story remember you're not alone. Talk to your parents, school counselor, or another concerned adult before doing anything rash.

If you or a loved one is experiencing any of these signs or symptoms, make an appointment with a physician as soon as possible. If you or a loved one is struggling with feelings of self-harm or suicide, seek medical attention immediately.

STOP focusing and planning on ending your life. Think about the people who love you or will miss you. They will help you to overcome negative influences in your life.

DROP all means you have for harming yourself. That includes pills, other drugs, weapons, anything and everything that can hurt you! That includes prescriptions that you may abuse.

LIVE by reaching out and allowing others to help you get beyond your hopelessness. There will be joy and peace in your life again. You are worth it! Suicide is a permanent solution to temporary circumstances.

Coach Lily says "Stop, Drop, and Live!"

WATCH FOR THESE DANGER SIGNS

You Should See Your Doctor If…

- You are feeling sad and hopeless nearly every day, for most of the day.

- You constantly feel irritable, sad, or angry.

- Nothing seems fun anymore—even the activities you used to love—and you just don't see the point of forcing yourself to do them.

- You feel bad about yourself—worthless, guilty, or just "wrong" in some way.

- You sleep too much or not enough.

- You've turned to alcohol or drugs to try to change the way you feel.

- You have frequent, unexplained headaches or other physical pains or problems.

- Anything and everything makes you cry.

- You're extremely sensitive to criticism.

- You've gained or lost weight without consciously trying to.

- You're having trouble concentrating, remembering things, thinking straight, and your grades may be plummeting because of it.

- You feel helpless and unable to meet your basic needs.

- You're thinking about death or suicide. (If so, talk to someone right away!)

There is ALWAYS another solution, even if you can't see it right now. Many people who have attempted suicide (and survived) say that they did it because they mistakenly felt there was no other solution to a problem they were experiencing. At the time, they could not see another way out, but in truth, they didn't really want to die. Remember that no matter how horribly you feel, these emotions will pass.

If your feelings are uncontrollable, tell yourself to wait 24 hours before you take any action. If you're afraid you can't control yourself, make sure you are never alone.

Problems and Solutions

Problem: Having a negative attitude and anticipating trouble is keeping you from being happy and this is affecting the people you interact with.

Solution: Make positivity a habit by planning ahead. Write down the typical things that stress you out and make plans to lessen that stress. Get help from a good friend to brainstorm multiple solutions, so you will always have an anti-negativity plan.

It has been proven that having a positive attitude has a direct connection with happiness and success.

Let's Summarize

STOP, DROP, AND LIVE!

Practice self-care in every area of your life. Don't let life just happen to you. You have the power to make choices that will safeguard your physical and mental health. Don't be afraid to ask for help. If your family and friends don't have the know-how to help you, be sure to reach out to professionals. If you find yourself sinking into negativity, remember to "Stop, Drop, and Live!"

Stop! Don't do it! Give yourself time to think. In a few more days or weeks, your entire life can change for the better. Stop focusing on the negative feelings. Concentrate on thoughts that make your life worth living. Your life is precious even if you don't feel that it is. Your feelings are temporary and will change. Your feelings do not always tell you the truth.

Drop! Put out the emotional fires. Get away from people, situations, or social media that may be causing you pain. Get rid of anything you may use to hurt yourself, preferably give it to a trusted friend or family member.

Live! Do not isolate yourself! Tell someone you need help. Call the suicide hotline, talk with a friend, a professional counselor, or any responsible adult. There are confidential and free options available to you.

Teen Assignment

Socialize, verbalize, improvise, visualize, exercise, and have fun. There are a host of activities to provide mental and physical stimulation. Find ways to incorporate exercise, games, and music into your daily life.

- View positive motivational videos.
- Memorize positive quotes and upbeat songs.
- Play online mind games.
- Change your environment
- Exercise to an online video
- Take your dog or a neighbor's dog for a walk
- Keep a gratitude journal.
- Reframe your challenges.

Parent-Teen Share

Help each other keep your bodies and mind healthy. A family that plays together is a happy family! Stay active together.

1. **Walking**. Take a relaxing stroll together in the evenings. You may talk, or you may choose not to talk. Just being together is the most important thing. Anything else may develop over time.

2. **Exercise or dance classes**. Many community centers offer free or low-cost activities. If you have space, you can start your own! Invite a few friends and their parents too.

3. **Singing**. Start a regular or impromptu family sing-along. Choose songs you all know and enjoy. You can set up a family playlist!

4. **Arts & Crafts**. Spend time creating together. Think of it as a time to relax, play, and share. You don't have to create a "work of art."

5. **Games: board games or cards**. You may choose games that allow you to talk about specific life choices. However, any game that you all enjoy will be a smart choice.

6. **Puzzles: jigsaw puzzles or crossword puzzles**. Two heads are better than one!

7. **Gardening**: Planting flowers and veggies in a raised flower bed is a purposeful activity that provides a sense of accomplishment. Eat and share these rewards with others.

REMEMBER

- Keep your body and mind healthy and success in all areas of life will follow!
- Keeping your mind and body healthy should be something you work on regularly.
- There are plenty of activities for all ages and levels of physical ability and all types of interests.

You just have to start!

13. Teenager's Guide to Depression: Tips and Tools for Helping Yourself or a Friend
<https://www.helpguide.org/articles/depression/teenagers-guide-to-depression.htm/>
13-2. Ibid

RESOURCES FOR YOU

National Suicide Prevention Lifeline: 1-800-273-TALK (8255)

Website: http://www.suicidepreventionlifeline.org

If you are in crisis, call this toll-free available 24 hours day, 7 days a week. The service is available to anyone. All calls are confidential. Visit their website for more details

Learn about other overcomers at this website:
https://suicidepreventionlifeline.org/stories/

Believe that life is worth living and your belief will help create the fact.
—William James

Chapter 12

Growing Up On Purpose

> *It is important to remember that conflict and tension are sources of growth, strength, and commitment.~ Joan Erikson*

WHAT IS A GROWN-UP?

Being a grown-up is based on different conditions depending on the culture or one's religion. In American society, we have more than one standard. However, there are two on which most people agree. One is based on the ages of 18 or 21 for different privileges, and the other is based on how well you handle life issues. According to psychologists, our emotional and psychological growth is caused by a different crisis at various stages of our lives. Opposing desires create each crisis. For example, you may have a desire to be taken care of and the desire to be independent at the same time. In most cases, it's not a winner-take-all situation; instead, there is a constant tension between the two desires. How well you learn to balance your opposing drives will demonstrate how grown-up you are. Your level of maturity is based on a few circumstances that are out of your control to some degree.

As our brains (cognitive ability), our experiences expand, and our bodies develop we become more capable of making the decision to grow up on purpose. However, you can make specific choices along the way that will play a major part in your growth. Growing up is about making wise decisions, so *you don't have to wait until you're older and smarter to be wise*."[14]

WHAT CAN I DO TO GROW UP?

First, you can decide on the values you want to live by. What are values? Values are your moral code. Values are the principles or standards of behavior that shows what is important in life to you. They are the rules you live by. We often adopt the rules and values of our parents, or society, but we are not limited to that. You can always choose to have higher goals. "When we know better, we do better." Most people believe the golden rule, "Treat others as you want to be treated" is the highest ideal. Your values are demonstrated by the importance you place on your different relationships, how you spend your money, the causes that you support, and how you use your time.

Secondly, you can decide to be a role model. Our society seems to be obsessed with celebrities and professional sports players as role models. Some have demonstrated great character traits; however, achieving wealth and fame may be enviable but neither are a reliable measure of a person's character. To be a role model means that you are a person who is looked to by others as an example to be imitated. This means you must have characteristics that any person can imitate if they put their mind to it. Everyone cannot be rich and famous, but we can all be kind and compassionate towards others. Our talents may not inspire people to chant our names, but we can make wise decisions about how to act and how to be responsible. You can inspire others by letting them see how you live your life. Just as we are all unique, we all have much in common as human beings. When others see your success, how you handle the triumphs and challenges of life with grace, you will inspire them to live their best life. To be a role model means that you demonstrate qualities such as a clear set of values, a commitment to your community, compassion, and the ability to overcome obstacles.

What is your commitment to your community? Our values can be seen in our day-to-day activities and interactions with others. When you are committed, you will feel a sense of responsibility and devotion which will drive your actions. It is easy and natural to be focused on our lives but when we decide to grow up, we begin to also focus on improving the lives of others. You will begin to see the needs that reach beyond yourself to recognize the needs of others. You may support causes such as the efforts of anti- human trafficking organizations or donating to homeless shelters. Are you family-oriented? Do you help the elderly or younger folk without being required to do it? Do you work to make new students feel at home? Age or financial status is not a factor when it comes to demonstrating your values. There are many ways that you can participate in your home, school, faith-based organizations, and in your community. After we adopt the rules that will help us to live our best life, our actions should demonstrate that consistently. You may struggle with this in the face of the many temptations and distractions in life, but overall, you want your life to stand for what you believe. Making choices that require that you give of your time, effort, and talents is a sign of maturity. It shows that you have made a choice to grow up.

Another marker of being a grown-up is how you overcome obstacles. It is easier to do the right thing when life is a bed of roses and everything is going your way, but how you handle difficulties is a sign of maturity. I, like many of you, thought that once I grew up, my life would be easier. Yes, you will be more in control of many aspects of your life. But remember some of those controls are meant to protect you while you mature. Adults can only do their part to prepare you. It is up to you to keep your mind alert, your eyes open, learn what you need to make the best decisions for your life. You should strive to have a good life. One aspect of growing up means taking proper steps and making sound decisions. However, there will always be obstacles, some small and some large. As you grow older, your problems will not end, but your ability to deal with them can get better. Taking the initiative to handle an issue before it becomes serious is a sign of growing up. Let's consider a story about a girl named "Sarah."

Sarah's Story

Sarah was an average teen with many influences floating around in her head about how to live her life. Sarah was luckier than most. She had a good homelife, friends, and supportive parents. Her basic needs were met and so were some of her wants. Yet, she still had to make decisions to stay "lucky" or she could make decisions that could lead to a more difficult path. She loved fashionable clothes and socializing with her friends. Most of the friends were in a club at school which required a certain grade point average.

One day, Sarah discovered that she had been so busy socializing that she was falling behind in her chemistry class. She may even fail if she didn't turn it around. She had to pass that class to maintain the grade she needed to stay in the club and to stay "part of the group." She told herself that her friends would still be her friends no matter what. She also knew it would be hard for them to socialize with her since so much of their time together was spent doing the required club activities at school and in the community when they weren't hanging out at the movies or putting together outfits when they visited each other on the weekends. Sarah had choices to make. She could continue with her enviable fashionista socializing lifestyle, fail chemistry, and hope that her friends would still have time for her. Or she could take steps to pass chemistry.

Sarah decided to discuss the situation with her counselor because she was not ready to share the "news" with her parents without a plan. The counselor gave Sarah some options: tutoring after school and student-to-student tutoring during school hours. Both would interfere with hanging out with her friends. It was a hard choice. Sarah decided that she needed to pass chemistry and keep her grades up for her future goals, not just to be a member of the club. She chose to receive both types of tutoring. She even asked the chemistry teacher if she could do any extra credit projects to improve her grade. As the weeks went on, Sarah did miss hanging out with her friends as much. But she was right, her loyal friends still made time for her, and they admired her decision. The limited time they did spend together was sweeter. When she completed the school year with a B-plus in chemistry, she was in the position to get scholarships to continue her education.

Sarah decided to grow up and see the big picture. This decision may have changed her entire life. (By the way, her parents were so impressed and proud of how Sarah overcame this obstacle that they trusted her more and that was reflected in their relationship and an increase in her allowance!) As Booker T. Washington once said, "Success is to be measured not so much by the position that one has reached in life as by the obstacles which one has overcome."

Every obstacle we face in life offers an opportunity for us to grow up. Remember that you do not have to do it alone. Adults and even your peers can help you to see things more clearly and help you to map out a plan to lessen negative effects or overcome an obstacle. Mind your business by paying attention and taking action for better outcomes. You will find others who want to help you. Be sure to return the favor to the universe by being willing to help someone who may need your help.

STILL NOT SURE HOW TO "CHOOSE" TO GROW UP!

Here are some basic guidelines to follow:

- Take responsibility for your actions
- Don't blame others for your mistakes
- Develop meaningful, balanced relationships
- Practice managing **all** your emotions.
- Learn to control negative emotions
- Make decisions that make you feel good about yourself

- Serve others or a greater good

- Become organized

- Don't always take the easy way out

- Set goals: personal, academic, career preparation, spiritual, etc.

- Give back to your community

- Find a mentor or mentors

- Ask for advice from wise people who care about you and are invested in your future

- Treat others the way you want to be treated

- Always do your best

- Apologize when you are wrong

- Negotiate when possible instead of always trying to win

- Decide what your core values are

- Maintain your core values no matter what

You may say, I want to do what is right, but I often fail. How can I develop a habit of choosing wisely? There is an old Cherokee tale about a man teaching his grandson about life. It goes like this, "A fight is going on inside me," he said to the boy." It is a terrible fight and it is between two wolves. One is evil – he is anger, envy, sorrow, regret, greed, arrogance, self-pity, guilt, resentment, inferiority, lies, false pride, superiority, and ego." He continued, "The other is good – he is joy, peace, love, hope, serenity, humility, kindness, benevolence, empathy, generosity, truth, compassion, and faith. The same fight is going on inside you – and inside every other person, too."

The grandson thought about it for a minute and then asked his grandfather, "Which wolf will win?" The old Cherokee simply replied, "The one you feed."

In other words, do those things that will support your better self. Choose the people who support you. Choose ideals that will strengthen you. Choose what you read, what you watch, what you expose your mind to if you want to grow up. Everyone faces similar challenges. We all may have a tendency to be selfish and unruly, but you can choose to live with order, joy, peace, and kindness. It is all in your hands to choose which part of yourself you want to increase or decrease. Respond to challenges with sound thinking, raise your values whenever possible. Expand your awareness of the world around you and develop the life skills that you will need as an adult.

There is a major difference in being childish and childlike. "Childish" usually refers to acting self-centered and unruly. Being "childlike" is seen as being somewhat innocent and amiable. As you grow older and wiser, you will want to be taken seriously by other adults and have more control over your life. To do that, you must exercise control over how you live starting from the inside out. How you think and feel decides how you act, how you are seen by others, and more importantly, how you feel about yourself. Take care of the better you and let the not-so-good you fall away.

Let's Summarize

You can choose to take deliberate steps to grow up. The sooner that you do, the more you can determine the outcome of your own life. Being a grown-up does not mean that you should not obey your parents or the rules of society. It means exactly the opposite.

A grown-up knows the value of following rules. A grown-up realizes that certain order is in place to protect us until we get more knowledge and experience. A grown-up understands we are all responsible for maintaining a polite, just society that protects and enhances the lives of all. The ability to be wise is learned behavior that you can start to practice at any age.

Being a grown-up does not come at a magical age. Some people of adult age have not truly become an adult. As a result, their lives are always a mess, from their personal lives to their careers. Some can handle one aspect of their life very well but not another. The key to becoming a well-rounded grown-up is to learn the skills and develop the attitudes that will keep you in balance. If you find that you don't have that balance, assess where you need help and get it.

Teen Assignment

Journal Activity: Write in your journal or in the space below. Imagine yourself 5 years from now with a good life. How old will you be then? Describe your life in terms of your personal, academic, career, financial future.

Your response may go beyond these questions, but here are some to think it through: What skills have you developed? What are you known for? What kind of friendships do you have? What you have accomplished. What goals do you have? What is your family life like? Imagine yourself in that moment in time and write as though you are there. What ways do you need to grow-up to have that life? Be as detailed as possible.

Write down the steps you will have to take to get to that life and any changes you will need to have that life in 5 years.

As you have time, go further into the future. Start a new entry and imagine yourself 20 years from now, then go back to 10 years. By completing the entry for "My Life in 20 Years" before "My Life in 10 Years," you can plan more effectively and realistically.

Remember to be as detailed as possible. You do not have to complete this at one sitting. But try to do it within 7 to 14 days after you begin. Revisit this exercise in six months or a year for a check up on how well you are doing or where you may need to step up your game.

You have the tools and the capability to create the life you want.

~Coach Lily

14. Grant, Adam. "How to Think Like a Wise Person" Psychology Today 28 August 2013/
<https://www.psychologytoday.com/us/blog/give-and-take/201308/how-think-wise-person>

My Life in Five Years   Age : _____

_____

_____

_____

_____

_____

_____

_____

_____

_____

_____

_____

_____

_____

_____

My Life in 10 Years   Age : _____

_____

_____

_____

_____

_____

_____

_____

_____

_____

_____

_____

_____

_____

_____

_____

_____

_____

_____

My Life in 20 Years   Age : _____

_____

_____

_____

_____

_____

_____

_____

_____

_____

_____

_____

_____

_____

_____

_____

_____

_____

Parent-Teen Share

Share your journal entry or read key parts of your entry to your parents or an adult mentor. Parents or adults should just listen at first. Then ask questions for clarification but try to not to make judgments. Together you can up with a few ways that can help now that will help you achieve your overall goals.

"I am a goal-achieving machine!"
—You

Goal 1:

_____

_____

_____

_____

How your parent/adult mentor will help:

_____

_____

_____

_____

_____

Goal 2:

_____

_____

_____

_____

How your parent/adult mentor can help:

_____

_____

_____

_____

Goal 3:

_____

_____

_____

_____

How your parent/adult mentor will help:

_____

_____

_____

_____

Writing Journal

Affirmations & Statements of Gratitude

_____

_____

_____

_____

_____

_____

_____

_____

_____

_____

_____

_____

_____

_____

_____

_____

_____

_____

_____

_____

_____

_____

_____

_____

_____

_____

Writing Journal

Affirmations & Statements of Gratitude

_____

_____

_____

_____

_____

_____

_____

_____

_____

_____

_____

_____

_____

_____

_____

_____

_____

_____

_____

_____

_____

_____

_____

_____

_____

_____

Writing Journal

Affirmations & Statements of Gratitude

_____

_____

_____

_____

_____

_____

_____

_____

_____

_____

_____

_____

_____

_____

_____

_____

_____

_____

_____

_____

_____

_____

_____

_____

_____

Writing Journal

Affirmations & Statements of Gratitude

_____

_____

_____

_____

_____

_____

_____

_____

_____

_____

_____

_____

_____

_____

_____

_____

_____

_____

_____

_____

_____

_____

_____

_____

_____

_____

_____

_____

Writing Journal

Affirmations & Statements of Gratitude

_____

_____

_____

_____

_____

_____

_____

_____

_____

_____

_____

_____

_____

_____

_____

_____

_____

_____

_____

_____

_____

_____

_____

_____

_____

_____

Writing Journal

Affirmations & Statements of Gratitude

_____

_____

_____

_____

_____

_____

_____

_____

_____

_____

_____

_____

_____

_____

_____

_____

_____

_____

_____

_____

_____

_____

_____

_____

_____

Writing Journal

Affirmations & Statements of Gratitude

_____

_____

_____

_____

_____

_____

_____

_____

_____

_____

_____

_____

_____

_____

_____

_____

_____

_____

_____

_____

_____

_____

_____

_____

_____

Writing Journal

Affirmations & Statements of Gratitude

_____

_____

_____

_____

_____

_____

_____

_____

_____

_____

_____

_____

_____

_____

_____

_____

_____

_____

_____

_____

_____

_____

_____

_____

_____

_____

Writing Journal

Affirmations & Statements of Gratitude

_____

_____

_____

_____

_____

_____

_____

_____

_____

_____

_____

_____

_____

_____

_____

_____

_____

_____

_____

_____

_____

_____

_____

_____

Writing Journal

Affirmations & Statements of Gratitude

_____

_____

_____

_____

_____

_____

_____

_____

_____

_____

_____

_____

_____

_____

_____

_____

_____

_____

_____

_____

_____

_____

_____

_____

_____

Writing Journal

Affirmations & Statements of Gratitude

_____

_____

_____

_____

_____

_____

_____

_____

_____

_____

_____

_____

_____

_____

_____

_____

_____

_____

_____

_____

_____

_____

_____

_____

Writing Journal

Affirmations & Statements of Gratitude

_____

_____

_____

_____

_____

_____

_____

_____

_____

_____

_____

_____

_____

_____

_____

_____

_____

_____

_____

_____

_____

_____

_____

_____

_____

Writing Journal

Affirmations & Statements of Gratitude

Writing Journal

Affirmations & Statements of Gratitude

_____

_____

_____

_____

_____

_____

_____

_____

_____

_____

_____

_____

_____

_____

_____

_____

_____

_____

_____

_____

_____

_____

_____

_____

_____

_____

Writing Journal

Affirmations & Statements of Gratitude

Writing Journal

Affirmations & Statements of Gratitude

_____

_____

_____

_____

_____

_____

_____

_____

_____

_____

_____

_____

_____

_____

_____

_____

_____

_____

_____

_____

_____

_____

_____

_____

_____

Writing Journal

Affirmations & Statements of Gratitude

_____

_____

_____

_____

_____

_____

_____

_____

_____

_____

_____

_____

_____

_____

_____

_____

_____

_____

_____

_____

_____

_____

_____

_____

Although no one can go back and make
a brand-new start,
Anyone can start from now and make a
brand-new ending!
—Carl Bard

Find a More Excellent Way!
—Coach Lily

Perfecting Destiny

Down East
Media & Publishing

Made in the USA
Las Vegas, NV
11 February 2022